Developing Enterprise iOS Applications

James Turner

O'REILLY®

Beijing · Cambridge · Farnham · Köln · Sebastopol · Tokyo

Developing Enterprise iOS Applications
by James Turner

Published by O'Reilly Media, Inc., 1005 Gravenstein Highway North, Sebastopol, CA 95472.

O'Reilly books may be purchased for educational, business, or sales promotional use. Online editions are also available for most titles (*http://my.safaribooksonline.com*). For more information, contact our corporate/institutional sales department: (800) 998-9938 or *corporate@oreilly.com*.

Editor:	Brian Jepson	**Cover Designer:**	Karen Montgomery
Production Editor:	Kristen Borg	**Interior Designer:**	David Futato
Proofreader:	O'Reilly Production Services	**Illustrator:**	Robert Romano

Revision History for the First Edition:

2011-12-13   First release

See *http://oreilly.com/catalog/errata.csp?isbn=9781449311483* for release details.

ISBN: 978-1-449-31148-3

[LSI]

1323440286

Table of Contents

Preface

Hello, and welcome to the exciting, frustrating, confusing, complex—and ultimately rewarding—world of Enterprise iOS development. This book attempts to distill the lessons learned from more than a year of on-the-ground experience, moving an Enterprise iOS application from first concept to shipping product. Hopefully, I can help you avoid some of the hidden coral reefs that lie beneath the Sea of Apple, and help you find the fair winds to keep your sails full.

The relationship between businesses and Apple has always been a complex one, partially due to Microsoft's traditional death-grip on the corporate market, and Apple's sometimes ambivalent attitude toward corporate users. iOS has done a lot to change this, as it brought many new Apple users in through the mobile back door. The reality is that iOS is something to be taken seriously by corporate IT departments, and the old "Blackberry or Bust" mentality is all but dead. This presents a huge opportunity for developers versed in both the Apple and Fortune 500 philosophies.

Who This Book Is For

First things first: if you've never touched Objective-C or Cocoa before, you need to backfill some knowledge before you jump into Enterprise iOS. There are any number of good books out there to get you started with the basic Apple development tools such as Xcode. One good place to start is *Learning iPhone Programming* by Alasdair Allan, also published by O'Reilly. Apple also provides a number of good resources to members of their developer community.

I'm also going to make the assumption in this book that you, the reader, are familiar with the ins and outs of Enterprise software development, including concepts such as SOAP, XML, REST, source control, continuous integration and regression, unit testing and code coverage, etc.

So, in short, this book is aimed at someone who expects to be (or already is) developing iOS software for use in Enterprise environments, and needs to know how to make the Apple development and deployment universe work smoothly with the requirements of corporate software methodologies. But many of the techniques laid out in this book may prove useful to you, even if you aren't in a large company or trying to sell applications to Enterprise customers.

How This Book Is Organized

To get you on your way, we'll start with a basic overview of the challenges that face Enterprise developers working with iOS. We will then, in turn, address each one of this issues, starting with collaborative development problems, and finishing up with long term support issues for Enterprise apps.

Along the way, we'll look at a number of the more important topics you may run into, including testing and distributing apps, integrating apps with backend systems, and a handy check-list of things you need to remember to think about as the ship date for your app approaches.

Each chapter stands more or less alone, so if you only want to see how to call a SOAP service from an iPhone app, you can jump right to that chapter without having to wade through all the other stuff.

Conventions Used in This Book

The following typographical conventions are used in this book:

Italic
> Indicates new terms, URLs, email addresses, filenames, and file extensions.

`Constant width`
> Used for program listings, as well as within paragraphs to refer to program elements such as variable or function names, databases, data types, environment variables, statements, and keywords.

`Constant width bold`
> Shows commands or other text that should be typed literally by the user.

`Constant width italic`
> Shows text that should be replaced with user-supplied values or by values determined by context.

> This icon signifies a tip, suggestion, or general note.

> This icon indicates a warning or caution.

Using Code Examples

This book is here to help you get your job done. In general, you may use the code in this book in your programs and documentation. You do not need to contact us for permission unless you're reproducing a significant portion of the code. For example, writing a program that uses several chunks of code from this book does not require permission. Selling or distributing a CD-ROM of examples from O'Reilly books does require permission. Answering a question by citing this book and quoting example code does not require permission. Incorporating a significant amount of example code from this book into your product's documentation does require permission.

We appreciate, but do not require, attribution. An attribution usually includes the title, author, publisher, and ISBN. For example: "*Developing Enterprise iOS Applications* by James Turner (O'Reilly). Copyright 2012 James Turner, 978-1-4493-1148-3."

If you feel your use of code examples falls outside fair use or the permission given above, feel free to contact us at *permissions@oreilly.com*.

Safari® Books Online

Safari Books Online is an on-demand digital library that lets you easily search over 7,500 technology and creative reference books and videos to find the answers you need quickly.

With a subscription, you can read any page and watch any video from our library online. Read books on your cell phone and mobile devices. Access new titles before they are available for print, and get exclusive access to manuscripts in development and post feedback for the authors. Copy and paste code samples, organize your favorites, download chapters, bookmark key sections, create notes, print out pages, and benefit from tons of other time-saving features.

O'Reilly Media has uploaded this book to the Safari Books Online service. To have full digital access to this book and others on similar topics from O'Reilly and other publishers, sign up for free at *http://my.safaribooksonline.com*.

How to Contact Us

Please address comments and questions concerning this book to the publisher:

O'Reilly Media, Inc.
1005 Gravenstein Highway North
Sebastopol, CA 95472
800-998-9938 (in the United States or Canada)
707-829-0515 (international or local)
707-829-0104 (fax)

We have a web page for this book, where we list errata, examples, and any additional information. You can access this page at:

http://shop.oreilly.com/product/0636920021759.do

In addition, there is a github repository that contains all the code and tools used in this book, organized by chapter. You can check a read-only copy out of github by using the repository address:

git://github.com/blackbear/enterprise-ios-applications.git

To comment or ask technical questions about this book, send email to:

bookquestions@oreilly.com

For more information about our books, courses, conferences, and news, see our website at *http://www.oreilly.com*.

Find us on Facebook: *http://facebook.com/oreilly*

Follow us on Twitter: *http://twitter.com/oreillymedia*

Watch us on YouTube: *http://www.youtube.com/oreillymedia*

Acknowledgments

I have been privileged to have had the opportunity to spend the last year and more developing a challenging enterprise application for a major company, and I wish that I could publicly recognize them for giving it to me. Alas, because of the realities of corporate PR policies and liabilities, I cannot. So I will have to instead recognize some of the people who have helped me on the way.

Firstly, I need to thank Jeff Delaney, who took a chance letting an inexperienced iOS developer drive an entire platform to delivery. I will be eternally grateful to him for giving me the chance.

I would have gotten nowhere without the rest of the mobile team: Anand Kolukula, Anton Spaans, Ashish Patel, Dan Nottingham, Eric Kampf, Girish Bhardwaj, Peter Floss, Sushil Kulkarni, and Vijay Hanumolu. Much of the section of build automation is there thanks to things I learned from Jill Warnshuis. Carl Belanger and Robert Boisse took over an efficiently operating group on short notice, and had the wisdom to let Manny be Manny. Thanks also to Dan and Girish for agreeing to review the book internally, and to Bill Bartow and Susan Rossnick for saying yes when they could have just as easily said no.

Brian Jepson is a really cool geek and God among Makers, as well as a friend. I was lucky to have him both acquire this book, and run with it as my editor. He's just one of the many people at O'Reilly I count as friends as well as colleagues, and that have made my many years doing projects with O'Reilly so enjoyable.

Both Daniel Steinberg and Alasdair Allan took time out of their busy schedules to take a look at a draft of the book and make suggestions (and make sure I didn't come off as a total raving maniac...). My deep appreciation to both of them.

I have to give a shout out to Apple, for creating such a wonderful environment to develop on. I give you guys a hard time, I know, but it's because I love your stuff and want it to be even better.

Finally, as always, my love and thanks to my wife Bonnie, and son Daniel. Without them, I wouldn't have the reason to get up in the morning and try to figure out how to make the UIAutomation Framework run.

CHAPTER 1

Enterprise iOS Applications

Enterprise application development is never a particularly fun endeavor. You tend to end up in large teams. There's lots of process to follow and layers of management all eager to make sure things are proceeding on course. There are lawyers who have to get involved with every piece of paperwork that you need signed. And, of course, you're frequently stuck having to slap a fresh coat of paint onto aging legacy software that can be fragile and difficult to interface with.

By contrast, the entire Apple development universe is about making thing fun and easy to use and producing eye-popping user interfaces that do incredible things. Unfortunately, when these two worlds collide, one or the other of the philosophies tends to end up on the losing end of the stick. Either you abandon all the practices that your management chain places such value in, and hope they can be understanding about it, or you have to sacrifice speed and functionality to appease the Gods of Process.

But there is a middle ground! Over the last year, I've been involved in a pioneering mobile application at a large, established software vendor. It's the first mobile product the company ever created, the first use of Apple technology by the company, and the first time Objective-C has ever found its way into the source control system. And in spite of the steep learning curve that was required to get the processes and people up to speed on the Way of Apple, we shipped on time and with a full feature set.

This book is an attempt to distill some of the lessons learned and best practices that we developed over that year (and continue to evolve as we head toward our 2.0 release). But before we jump in to the nuts and bolts of iOS development in an enterprise environment, it's worth noting some of the reasons that it can be such a difficult effort.

Apple Developers—An Army of One

To start with, the Apple model of development, as embodied by Xcode, strongly favors a single developer model. That isn't to say that it is impossible to create applications using concurrent development, and in fact, recent versions of Xcode have drastically improved support for source control and merging. But the project-central nature of

Xcode makes it easy for people working on the same project to get out of sync with each other, and some resources such as translation files are almost impossible to jointly develop, for reasons that you'll see in the next chapter, on concurrent development.

There are tricks you can use, involving the new Workspace features that were introduced in Xcode 4, as well as splitting out code with static libraries, that can make your code more modular and amenable to simultaneous development by more than one coder. We'll talk about those in depth in Chapter 2.

Build Automation Is a Bit of a Challenge

Apple has a very specific view of how applications should be developed, at least if you take Xcode as a guidepost to their philosophy. While Java developers, for example, have spent years using tools such as Hudson and Ant to automate the compilation, unit testing and deployment of their applications, Xcode puts it all under one roof. This is great if you're flying solo: you can compile, test and archive your code with a push of a button. But if you want to employ continuous regression testing, you need to really work at it. The same goes for building and packaging Ad Hoc builds for testers. In most big companies, handing out binaries that you compiled on your development machine won't win you many friends.

There are ways that you can compile and test from the command line, and even integrate Xcode builds into integration tools such as Hudson. Some of them are even officially supported! In Chapter 3, you'll see how you can create a reliable continuous integration system, and learn what you can and can't do with it.

Objective-C Doesn't Play Well with Others

Enterprises love SOAP. It has built in support through frameworks such as CXF and JAX-WS for Java, and .NET developers can leverage the rich support for SOAP in modern versions of Visual Studio.

The iPhone and its cousins support it not a whit. Unless you want to construct your XML by hand, there is no native support for SOAP in iOS. Even the XML support in iOS is a pure pull parser model, when what you frequently want is a DOM parser. Thankfully, iOS has finally introduced support for JSON in iOS 5!

Luckily, there are good third-party libraries for most of these, even SOAP. If you're willing to make use of open source libraries, you can talk to just about anything from iOS, although it may take a bit of work.Chapter 4 looks at how to talk to SOAP, REST, JSON and pure XML backend servers.

Code Coverage Is for Weenies

Does your company use Coverity to measure code complexity? Super, but Objective-C isn't supported! What do you do when your manager asks you for code coverage figures on your OCUnit tests, something that was broken for most of iOS 4 and just came back to life in iOS 5? Smiling and offering chocolate chip cookies is only going to get you so far.

Xcode and Objective-C are often the odd man out in enterprise development. Outside of the Xcode tool chain, there's little to no commercial support for the language. And the tools built into Xcode have a habit of breaking between releases. UIAutomation broke for a while in early Xcode 4 builds, and there are features still limping along in it, a year later.

By picking and choosing (and with a little elbow grease), you can get most of the metrics that your company might demand of you. Chapter 5 takes you through code coverage, CCN metrics, and other associated issues with testing.

iTunes Connect Is a Great Way to Keep Your Legal Staff Employed

Ever had to run a contract through your legal department? Are you still waiting to get it back? Before you can do anything with products in iTunes, there's a passel of paperwork you'll need to wade through, especially if you plan to charge for your app. There are also ongoing issues that you should think about and discuss with your management before embarking on an iOS development project.

Beyond that, there are questions you'll need to think about in regards to internationalization, product messaging (at which point marketing will get involved), how to demonstrate the product, and a host of other issues to consider. Chapter 6, although by no means a comprehensive checklist, does try to hit the high points on what to watch out for as you move your product into the store.

You Can Have Any Style of Distribution, as Long as it's iTunes

Now we come to the most interesting issue, as far as enterprise distribution goes. Apple, unlike the other mobile platforms, has a "my way or the highway" approach to application distribution. You can put your app in the store, distribute it in-house with major restrictions, create an Ad Hoc build for up to 100 devices, distributing it inside your own company using an Enterprise license, and...well, that's it. Significantly, there's no way for a developer to create an application for a diverse population of customers that they can install directly, without downloading it directly from the App Store.

For companies used to shipping code and managing stock, the iTunes ways of life is going to come as a bit of a shock. Getting a product up and released through the store is a delicate dance that needs to be well planned, especially if you need to hit a launch date precisely. Because of the "only ever one version in the store" reality, you need to think carefully about how to manage client-server version mismatches. If you're going to use Ad Hoc provisioning for your testers, you can end up spending half your life managing the UDID list in iTunes, so that the app can be tested on a new device. Enterprise licenses can relieve a lot of this headache, but they come with their own complications, including having to juggle keychains to create your builds.

There's only so far that technology can help with these problems; strategy may prove a better ally. Chapter 7 talks about how to provision and distribute your application without going insane, and the hard decisions you may have to end up making.

The Road Is Long and Winding

Just because you have your first release out doesn't mean your headaches are over. When dealing with client-server architectures, it's important that the client and server stay in sync, and that's hard when iTunes insists that you can only have one version of your software available for sale at any one time.

Chapter 8 deals with the travails of maintaining iOS applications over the long haul, and offers some strategies for how to attack the problem.

A Few Caveats

Given the glacial pace of the Java Community Process, you can write about Java development without much fear the language is going to slip out from under you overnight. Objective-C is much more...dynamic.

It is almost a sure thing that something (or several somethings) discussed in this book will be overtaken by changes to the development environment. It's as up to date as I can make it, especially in reference to the recent release of iOS 5. Note that because people are still discovering how some things have changed (for the good or not) in iOS 5, it's possible that there will be information that will need to be updated in the errata (see *http://shop.oreilly.com/product/0636920021759.do*) or future reprints as things move forward. Honestly, iOS is always a moving target, both from a development and licensing standpoint.

Also, although I may talk about something as a best practice, your mileage may vary. Different companies have different comfort levels about change. Company A might be fine with using git as a source control system, while company B insists on CVS. You're going to need to temper the desire to "do the right thing" with the realities of how your workplace operates.

Finally, this is not a general book on Objective-C and iOS best practices. In particular, I'm going to be doing the bare minimum as far as UI treatments go. There are a ton of good books on how to make beautiful iOS applications, and this book isn't about that. It's about the messy backend and logistical stuff that makes Enterprise applications work. Doing a lot of cavorting with `UIViewContainers` would only clutter up the program listings, and distract from the code and concepts I'm trying to highlight.

For the same reason, you won't see me running a lot of strings through localization, and I may even (gasp) forget to do the right thing with retain and release on occasion (not that this will matter any more, once people have cut over to the automatic reference count compiler!) I'm going to assume you know how to do both, and I'm going to try to emphasize code clarity rather than pristine correctness.

Now that you know all the reasons that iOS enterprise development can drive you nuts, let's go through each of the problems, chapter by chapter, and see what we can't do to improve things.

CHAPTER 2

Concurrent Development with iOS

Enterprise application development at most companies is usually about teams, often large teams. The Agile movement has done little to change this tendency, and in fact embraces the idea of team development, with a backlog of stories that are apportioned out to the pool of developers on the team on a sprint by sprint basis.

So what does this mean for iOS applications development? Well, if you're a Java programmer working in Eclipse, you can split up development pretty easily. Eclipse is largely directory based, and the Eclipse project file is fairly stable. Xcode...not so much. Xcode is the obsessive-compulsive poster child of IDEs. It wants to manage every single file at a micromanager level, and it's not enough to drop new files into a directory, you need to tell Xcode to use them in specific build targets, and all of that info is stored in a single *xcodeproj* file.

If you're not very careful when creating new files in Xcode, you tend to end up with everything in one flat directory. Using groups can give structure to the project view inside Xcode, but it does nothing to organize the physical file system layout. And as you may have already discovered, trying to go in after the fact and move files around on disk is messy, because there's no way to notify Xcode that you're doing it. The best I've ever done is to delete the references (which turn red when you move the files), then re-add them and hope that you haven't screwed up your build manifests in the process.

A Little Ditty 'bout Tom and Diane

Let's look at a very small project with two developers, and see how things can get messy very quickly. We'll be developing a social networking tool throughout the book, and our two developers (Tom and Diane) are going to start with the login screen. Tom is in charge of UI, and Diane with backend integration. Unfortunately, Tom and Diane work for BuggyWhipCo, which is still using (shudder) CVS as the source management platform, which isn't supported natively by Xcode. As of this writing, Xcode only supports git and Subversion natively in the UI, so our intrepid pair is going to have to check their code in manually on the command line. This is not at all uncommon—git is extremely rare in corporate settings, although SVN is becoming more popular. Many companies are using proprietary tools from companies such as IBM. The source control system at the company I spend my days coding for uses a source control system used by so few companies that telling you the name of the tool would literally let you figure out where my day job is.

Tom begins by creating an CVS repository for the project, and then fires up Xcode, and creates a new project using the Xcode project wizard, specifying a master-detail style application (see Figure 2-1).

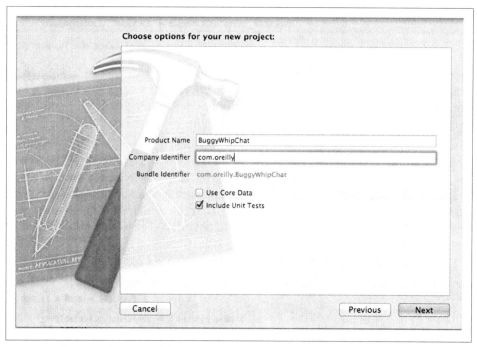

Figure 2-1. Creating the BuggyWhipChat project

Before he does anything else, he checks in the project by importing it into CVS:

```
Tom$ cvs import buggywhipchat buggywhipco v1-0
.
.
.
No conflicts created by this import
Tom$
```

Tom gives Diane the location of the new repository, and she checks out the project to start adding some backend server integration. She starts by creating an stub class that she plans to check in immediately, so that Tom can start coding against the interface, even before Diane has implemented it. She uses Xcode to create some Twitter API methods (don't panic, we're not going to try to implement a real Twitter interface in this book; it would take up the whole thing!) Figure 2-2 shows what her Xcode environment looks like after creating a class, in a new group called APIs.

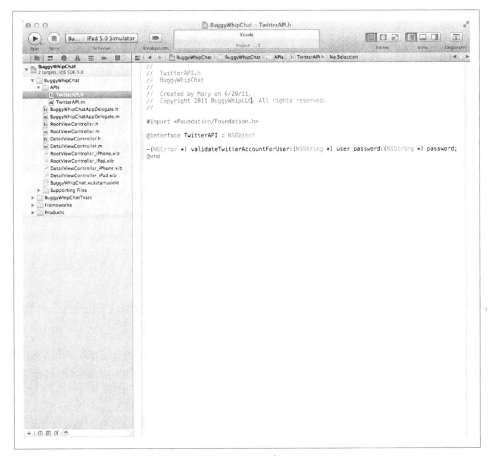

Figure 2-2. The project view after adding Diane's new files

Meanwhile, unbeknownst to Diane, Tom has begun working on his UI design. In support of it, he has created a splash screen using an XIB file. His project view is shown in Figure 2-3.

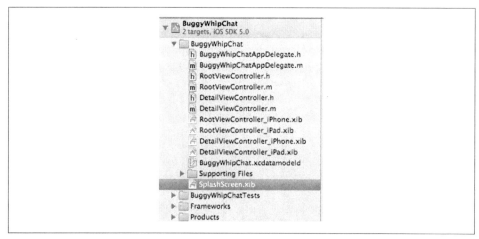

Figure 2-3. Tom's project with the new XIB file

At this point, everything is in place for hilarious hijinks to ensue. Let's say that Diane checks her new code into CVS first:

```
Diane$ cvs add BuggyWhipChat/BuggyWhipChat/TwitterAPI.*
cvs add: scheduling file `BuggyWhipChat/BuggyWhipChat/TwitterAPI.h' for addition
cvs add: scheduling file `BuggyWhipChat/BuggyWhipChat/TwitterAPI.m' for addition
cvs add: use `cvs commit' to add these files permanently
```

This isn't the whole story though, because if Diane commits now, she'll be also committing changes to a local file that got silently modified when she added those class files to Xcode. A *cvs status* invocation tells the whole story:

```
cvs status: Examining BuggyWhipChat/BuggyWhipChat.xcodeproj
===============================================================
File: project.pbxproj   Status: Locally Modified
```

That pesky project file has also been modified, since it keeps track of which files are associated with which targets in the project. If Diane did not commit the changes to the file, anyone else checking out the project won't see the new class in their project view, even though the files will physically be on the disk.

Let's say that Diane has done this enough times that she remembers to commit the project file. We're not out of the woods yet! What's going to happen when Tom wants to commit his new XIB file? Being an experienced CVS user, he's going to start by doing a *cvs update*:

```
cvs update: Updating buggywhipchat/BuggyWhipChat/BuggyWhipChat.xcodeproj
1.1.1.1
retrieving revision 1.2
Merging differences between 1.1.1.1 and 1.2 into project.pbxproj
rcs merge: warning: conflicts during merge
```

Well, that's no fun at all...not only do you end up with a merge conflict, but because of the way CVS does merges, you end up with a broken project file (which is likely to crash Xcode if you happen to have the project open at the time you do the merge). Opening the file reveals the conflicts, which will occur in several sections. Here's an example (the lines have been truncated for readability):

```
<<<<<<< project.pbxproj
1A05AE0613BB5F880080AAD4 /* SplashScreen.xib */ = ...
=======
1A05AE1213BB63210080AAD4 /* TwitterAPI.h */ = ...
1A05AE1313BB63210080AAD4 /* TwitterAPI.m */ = ...
>>>>>>> 1.2
```

So, Tom is going to get to edit his *project.pbxproj* file by hand, looking for the conflicts and resolving them. In this case, it's pretty simple, because he can just take the changes made from both sides, ending up with the project view shown in Figure 2-4.

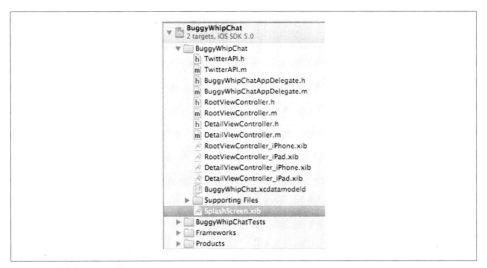

Figure 2-4. The merged project view

More Merge Mayhem

"OK," you may be saying to yourself, "It's messy, but I can deal with doing some merging every time someone adds new files to the project." But adding files is just the beginning of your troubles. The project file is changed whenever you change the build target in Xcode. It gets changed if you update your provisioning profile. Adding a group, moving files between groups—you name it, and it somehow is going to mess with the project file.

You can end up with all sorts of disasters if you merge the project file incorrectly, from broken builds to projects that won't open at all inside Xcode. They are far from human-readable, although once you've had to deal with enough merge issues, you start to get the lay of the land a bit.

This isn't some abstract peril. Because of the way my company uses Agile development, I may be working on multiple headlines at the same time, and I'm not allowed to promote the code associated with a headline to the QA branch until the headline is complete. As a result, I frequently have multiple sub-branches of the project living in separate checked out copies of the workspace on my desktop, and promote and merge as appropriate. If I had a dollar for every time that I broke the parent build by mis-merging the project files, I could buy myself a nice dinner.

But at least there's a chance that you can merge project files, since they're vanilla XML. Let's talk about a real nightmare: language translation files. The espoused best practice when doing iPhone development is to use *NSLocalizedString* to do all your string look-ups, and then let *genstrings* autogenerate the translation resource files (which are all bundled together under the *Localizable.strings* file in your Xcode project). As experienced iOS developers learn, *genstrings* overwrites the old translations every time you use it, so there are a number of publicly available tools that will do a more graceful regeneration and merge. My tool of choice is the Python script *localize.py*, available at *http://github.com/joaomoreno/Green-Apples/raw/master/localize.py*.

As long as you only have a single person dealing with this file, you're OK. But once you have multiple people all adding strings, or even multiple branches (as in my situation with multiple branches for different headlines), you're sunk! The big problem you're going to run into is that the translation files are UTF-16 files, and most source control systems blithely look at them, and say "Oh, that's a binary file; I have no idea how to merge it." So if you have multiple people messing around with your translation strings, you can end up with a very painful manual merge (or have to use a tool such as *File-Merge*, which knows how to handle UTF-16 files).

In general, any machine-generated iOS file (XIB files, core data schemas, etc.) is going to be a headache to merge if you have more than one person mucking with them at the same time, and the cost of doing it wrong can be very high. So how do you handle multiple engineer development without going prematurely grey?

Workspaces and Static Libraries

One of the major advancements that Xcode 4 brought with it was the concept of a workspace. You can think of workspaces as a project composed of projects, and one of the big benefits of this approach is that each project tracks its files and other settings separately. What this means is that Diane can add classes to her API project, and Tom can merrily design UI, without stepping on each other's projects.

You can create a new workspace-based project by simply selecting *File→New→Work-space*, but assuming that you've already got a project underway, you can turn your existing project into a workspace-based project by doing *File→Save as Workspace...* Once you have saved your project as a workspace, you can open it by selecting the *xcworkspace* file using *File→Open*.

As I mentioned, the big advantage of using workspaces is that you can create multiple projects under the workspace, and have the main project set dependencies on the "child" projects, so that they are automatically built and linked in to the main project. But because they use independent project files, developers can work on them individually without creating merge issues.

Let's assume that Diane did just that, and turned her project into a workspace. In addition, she created a new project inside the workspace called ChatAPI. To do that, all she needed to do is to choose *File→New→Project*, and once she was at the new project wizard, select a Cocoa Static Touch Library under the iOS Framework & Library section. She named it ChatAPI, and placed the project directory at the same level as the main BuggyWhipChat workspace file (see Figure 2-5).

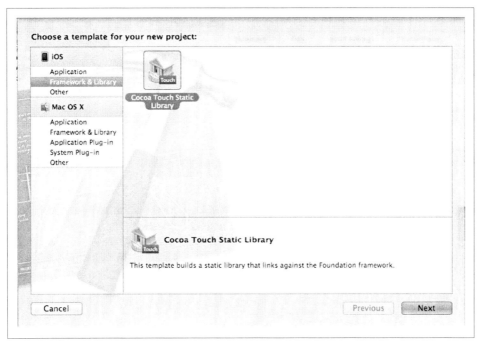

Figure 2-5. Creating a project inside a workspace

When she's done, she ends up with a project navigator view that looks something like the one in Figure 2-6.

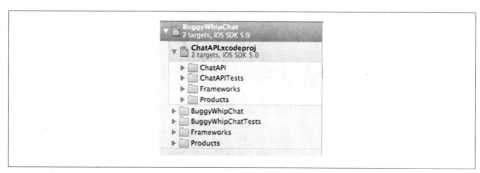

Figure 2-6. The project view of a workspace with a subproject

What this looks like on the file system, in an abbreviated form, is this:

```
./BuggyWhipChat
./BuggyWhipChat/BuggyWhipChat
./BuggyWhipChat/BuggyWhipChat/DetailViewController.h
./BuggyWhipChat/BuggyWhipChat/DetailViewController.m
./BuggyWhipChat/BuggyWhipChat/RootViewController.h
./BuggyWhipChat/BuggyWhipChat/RootViewController.m
./BuggyWhipChat/BuggyWhipChat/TwitterAPI.h
./BuggyWhipChat/BuggyWhipChat/TwitterAPI.m
./BuggyWhipChat/BuggyWhipChat.xcodeproj
./ChatAPI
./ChatAPI/ChatAPI
./ChatAPI/ChatAPI.xcodeproj
./ChatAPI/ChatAPI.xcodeproj/project.pbxproj
```

Diane also needs to make the main project depend on the new ChatAPI project. There are a few ways to do this, but probably the easiest is to select the BuggyWhipChat project, go to the Build Phases view, and add ChatAPI as a target dependency. Xcode is supposed to figure this out automatically, but I've had hit-or-miss luck with it, so I prefer to do it explicitly. While she's there, she also has to add the library archive from the subproject as a linked library for the main project (see Figure 2-7).

Also, somewhat annoyingly, Diane has to manually add a relative path to the ChatAPI directory to the `Header Search Paths` build setting for the parent project, so that the parent can reference any new header files that Diane creates after the split. Or, alternatively, she can copy the header files into the main project, although this will get you back into the scenario of having two people modifying the same project file.

The final step is to move the TwitterAPI source and header into the new subproject, and remove the references from the main project. Because Xcode associates projects and groups with physical location on disk, they're going to still be in the BuggyWhipChat directory. If you're obsessive (or your company is) about directory organization, you'd probably want to move the files physically to the correct directory, and use *Add Files...* to recreate the references in the ChatAPI project.

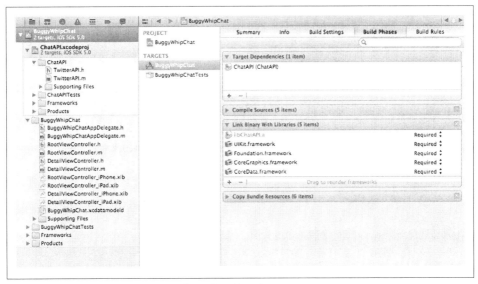

Figure 2-7. Making the main project depend on the subproject

Diane can then check her new workspace and project into CVS by adding all the new files and commit the other ones. Tom does a CVS update, and importantly, reopens the project using the workspace file. Now both Tom and Diane are working inside a common workspace, but on different project files.

So what happens if Tom and Diane both independently create new files now? As an example, suppose that Diane adds a new Objective-C class called `GoogleTalkAPI`, while Tom creates a new `UIViewController`-based class called `ChatChooser`, complete with an XIB file. This time, Tom is the first one to add and commit his new files. When Diane does a CVS update, here's what she sees (in abridged form):

```
Dianescvs Diane$ cvs update buggywhipchat
cvs update: Updating buggywhipchat/BuggyWhipChat/BuggyWhipChat
U buggywhipchat/BuggyWhipChat/BuggyWhipChat/ChatChooser.h
U buggywhipchat/BuggyWhipChat/BuggyWhipChat/ChatChooser.m
U buggywhipchat/BuggyWhipChat/BuggyWhipChat/ChatChooser.xib
cvs update: Updating buggywhipchat/BuggyWhipChat/BuggyWhipChat.xcodeproj
U buggywhipchat/BuggyWhipChat/BuggyWhipChat.xcodeproj/project.pbxproj
```

The files that Tom modified (the project file, when he added new classes) and the new class files and XIB have shown up. Notice that even though Diane has added new files to her project as well, there's no conflict, because those files were added to the project file for the ChatAPI project. In fact, once she adds and commits her files, Tom will get a similar experience the next time he updates:

```
buggywhipchat Tom$ cvs update
cvs update: Updating ChatAPI
cvs update: Updating ChatAPI/ChatAPI
U ChatAPI/ChatAPI/GoogleTalkAPI.h
U ChatAPI/ChatAPI/GoogleTalkAPI.m
```

```
cvs update: Updating ChatAPI/ChatAPI.xcodeproj
U ChatAPI/ChatAPI.xcodeproj/project.pbxproj
```

No muss, no fuss, no broken project files. This strategy works well for dividing up work, with a few caveats.

Make Sure All Dependent Projects Do Their Own Unit Testing

Xcode will offer to create a Unit Test target for a library, when you create it. You should take Xcode up on the offer. By its nature, a dependent library needs to be able to stand alone, and that includes testing.

This is pretty straightforward if all your library does is implement business logic, or something else divorced from the UI. It becomes more troublesome if you are going to try, for example, to divide up the UI responsibilities for the applications into various subprojects, and then integrate them all up into a main project. In iOS 5, you can do business level testing by injecting your unit tests into the running application, but in this case, you need to have an operating UIApplicationDelegate. Where are your subprojects going to get it? Are you going to have a dummy *main.m* in each of your subprojects that fires up the application just far enough to test the UI code? These are the kinds of issues you need to consider when you start dividing up your project.

Also, as mentioned in the next section, XIBs and other resources can't live in libraries, so the ability to divide up UI work into multiple developers is fairly limited to begin with.

You Need to Plan Out Common Resource Issues

Unfortunately, breaking projects up into subprojects doesn't solve all your problems. In fact, it doesn't solve many of them. For example, there's no way in a static library to include bundle information, such as localizable strings and images. You need a framework to do that, and at the moment, Apple doesn't allow custom frameworks for the iOS family of products. Maybe sometime in the future, this will be available, but for the moment, you're fairly much screwed if you want to keep your localizations close to the library.

This doesn't mean that you can't take advantage of NSLocalizedString in your libraries, just that the actual *Localized.strings* files are going to have to live in the main project. And as I mentioned, those files are a real bear to merge, because they are UTF-16 format. The best strategy is going to depend on the dynamics of the group, but it probably makes sense to appoint a single "stringmeister," who is responsible for the overall coordination of the string files. This person can also serve as a liaison to the translation resources (in-house or contracted) that are actually going to do the work.

This is also a good practice because, in the absence of a single person riding herd on the strings, you tend to end up with duplication all over the place as multiple developers add strings such as "OK" and "Cancel." It is, however, a thankless job, so it's probably a good idea to rotate the work around to the various members of the team.

The biggest problem you're going to face is that you can't put XIB files in your libraries, because only framework libraries can hold this kind of data, and Apple reserves to itself the ability to create frameworks in iOS.

Libraries Aren't Entirely Useless!

So what *are* static libraries good for? As it turns out, quite a lot! For example, in the application I developed, there is a lot of code around parsing XML returned from the server, and the code that handles the network communications themselves. It is all abstracted away from the UI, so it could easily by placed into a separate static library that other iOS applications could use, and I could maintain it without stepping on (for example) someone developing a new iPad application. You need to think out how you want to divide up your application to avoid circular libraries dependencies, although the `@class` hack can be used to handle class references between libraries, if you must. This involves putting an `@class` annotation at the top of a header file to inform the compiler that a class is defined in another file, without actually including that file. It's the same way you avoid circular references to classes in header files.

The other advantage of static libraries is that it allows you to treat them differently, from a build perspective. When might this be useful? Well, I recently converted our application over to the automatic reference count compiler added in iOS 5. However, I depend on several third-party packages that are problematic to convert over because of the way they directly manipulate low-level system objects. I could have tried to puzzle it out, but because of the licenses involved, I would have had to involve our legal department because I would have been required to contribute the changes back to the open source projects involved. While I don't have a philosophical objection to doing that, it was more hassle than I had time to deal with at the moment.

However, by putting each of the third-party libraries into their own static library, I was able to choose at ARC conversion time whether or not I wanted each of the libraries to be converted. By saying no, I was able to convert the main application without having to modify the libraries.

There are other times when you might need different build settings for a library, such as compiler optimization levels, additional compiler flags, etc. Static libraries let you easily segregate portions of your application so that you can do just these kinds of things.

You Can Still End Up Stepping on Each Other's Feet

The other headache you can run into is that, at the end of the day, there are still some code paths that everyone is going to end up going through. For example, a main menu that leads to the various subfunctions of the application will need to be modified by each developer working on a subfunction, to enable access to that function. But this is not nearly as bad a problem as adding and removing files, because if you're only editing a class file, you're not modifying the project file, so you're left with an ordinary merge, just like in any other language under source control.

However, it's also possible to modify your project file without meaning to. Many activities that take place on the project view edit the project file under the table. For example, if you set `NSZombieEnable`, you've just tweaked the project file. If you check it in, you're going to end up in merge mayhem. So, a general rule of thumb is, don't check in your project file on a commit, unless you've added or removed files (or made some change to the project that needs to be permanent, such as adding a framework).

Luckily, a lot of the things you can change (such as the current build target) are stored in the user project file, not the project-wide file. These files live in the *xcuserdata* directory inside of *xcodeproj*. There's a separate data directory for each user (*Diane.xcuserdatad*, for example), so you would be unlikely to create a conflict even if the files did get checked into source control, but there's no reason they should be checked in at all, so don't. In fact, if you're lucky enough to be able to use XCode's integrated SVN or git support, it won't even offer to check these files in unless you force it to.

Let's Be Careful Out There

Best practices are great, but they never take the place of diligence and planning. As hard as you try, if you have multiple people working on the sample iOS project, files will get broken, builds will fail, and work may get lost.

To some extent, these are the rules of the road when working on iOS. You don't have Frameworks to let you cleanly divide up work, Xcode is highly dependent on machine-generated files to manage the project, and none of it was designed to facilitate team-based application development.

However, going in to the project knowing where the pitfalls are likely to occur is a big first step toward preventing problems. Nothing, however, takes the place of good communications between team members. Leverage those agile practices, mention during your standup if you plan to mess around with a frequently touched file. If there are geographic issues with your team, make sure you have procedures in place for good hand-offs, so your current state follows the sun as well as your code.

One method of catching problems you may have introduced (before they can fester) is continuous integration and automated builds. In the next chapter, we'll walk through the challenges that build automation presents, and see how (relatively) easy it is to get out of the nightly build game.

CHAPTER 3

Automating iOS Builds

One of the constants of the Enterprise universe is that, almost before you have your first line of code written, someone will be asking you to set up automated nightly builds with regression testing. And I'm not disagreeing with the practice, because nothing will get a project in trouble faster than the "it worked on my desktop" syndrome. Automated builds are a good way to keep developers honest, and they also can provide a single place for your testing team to get builds to bang on.

And the good news is, with a little bit of finesse, you can get your iOS builds automated, and never have to worry about it again. Apple doesn't make it easy to do, not so much because the tools aren't there, but that it can be a scavenger hunt through forums, sparse documentation, and third-party web-sites to find out exactly how to make it tick. What we'll do in this chapter is to go through the entire process from start to end, so that hopefully you can do it without having to dive into all the research.

Introducing Hudson

There are no lack of build automation systems available these days, and any attempt to cover them all would be far outside the scope of this book. Instead, we'll look at one popular, open-source build system, called Hudson. Java developers are probably familiar with Hudson, since it is one of the leading tools for build automation in that space. But Hudson can be used for just about any type of build, and if you haven't already chosen a system, I'd make a strong recommendation for Hudson. But regardless of what build system you plan to use, the tips about how to execute builds from the command line (which is the heart of automating an iOS build) should be valid.

Hudson was pioneered at Sun, and was acquired by Oracle as part of their purchase of Sun. Due to some political turmoil between Oracle and the Hudson developer community, a forked version of Hudson called Jenkins was created, which is (for the moment) entirely compatible with Hudson. In the summer of 2011, Oracle donated Hudson to the Eclipse Foundation—whether this will allow a reconciliation with the Jenkins crowd is yet to be seen.

Hudson is written in Java, and although it isn't required, prefers to use the Ant build tool as the method to execute builds. Since Ant can do just about anything, including running command line scripts, it is a totally reasonable choice for automating iOS builds.

Breaking the News to Your IT Department

Maybe you're one of the lucky few, and your company has fully embraced the Apple work, with Mac Pros and Macbooks as far as the eye can see. More likely, you're living in la vida Microsoft, with a purchasing department used to buying low-priced Wintel boxes whenever anyone needs a development machine, and perhaps a Dell or HP server when you need a heavy-duty build machine.

If you've started doing iOS development inside your company, and you're not using personal equipment, you've probably already had to break the news to them that you can only really develop iOS applications on Apple hardware (we'll ignore the world of the Hackintosh, as that's even less likely to meet with approval from IT than true Apple gear).

Well, now you get to go back to them and explain that if they want automated builds, they're going to have to go back to their piggy-bank and pony up the funds for another Mac of some variety, because you can't build iOS applications on anything but a Mac either. Unless you're doing an absurdly large amount of builds, you don't need much of one though. At my day job, we do just fine with a mid-range iMac, reserving the heavy-duty Mac Pros for developers. In fact, this one machine is now running not only our iOS builds (for about 10 different code branches), but also our Android, Blackberry and J2ME feature phone builds!

There are rumblings that there may be ways soon to run Mac OS X Server in a virtual environment on non-Apple hardware, so that's something to keep an eye out for, but at the moment, you should start getting the hardware for a dedicated build machine in the purchasing pipeline if you expect to do automated builds. For the same reason that having developers produce builds is a bad idea, running automated builds on a machine that is also used for development is a bad idea.

Provisioning Your Build Machine

Before we get into the nuts and bolts of setting up Hudson, we need to make sure that the basics for iOS development are available on your new server. Primarily, this means installing the latest production version of Xcode. You can either copy the disk image that you used to install Xcode on your development machine, or download a fresh copy from the iOS Developer Site. You can now also buy a copy of XCode via the Mac App store.

A quick note about version compatibility of Xcode is worth mentioning here. At one point, Apple had Xcode 3.2, Xcode 4.0 and a beta of Xcode 4.1 all available for download at the same time from the developer site. It is easy to imagine that you could end up with situations where developers were using one version of Xcode, while the build machine was running a different version.

By and large, this is not an issue. While you never want to have your build machine running a beta version of Xcode (you can't upload apps built with it to the App Store, for one thing), I've generally found that Xcode has been fairly forgiving of mix and match Xcode versions dealing with the same project files. The big (and nasty) exception is that if you use features that are only available in the beta, and then try to open the project in an older version, anything could happen. But, for example, at the moment I am developing at home using the latest Xcode beta, checking in my files and having them work without a hitch in Xcode 4.1 on our build machine. The one big gotcha is that you may want to start building using the GM version a week or so before the new version of iOS is released, so you can have a version in the store at launch time. If you bought your copy of XCode via the Mac App store, rather than downloading it from the developer portal, you won't be able to update it until the new version of XCode is formally released.

The other (and unpleasant) things you'll need to keep in sync between development and build machines are the provisioning profiles and certificates. There are a number of reasons that these can go out of sync. For one, every time you add someone to your Ad Hoc profile (which will be discussed in more detail in Chapter 7), you end up with a new profile, which you need to reference in your project file. If your build machine doesn't have a copy of this profile (or the backing certificate) in the keychain, the build will fail. We'll discuss this later in this chapter in more detail. If you're doing both an Enterprise and Ad Hoc/App Store build, things can get very, very complicated, because of keychain conflicts. This is also discussed in Chapter 7.

Installing Hudson

Once you have Xcode installed and running (a good test is to check out your project as a logged in user on the build machine, and make sure that you can build and run the app), it's time to install the build automation tool (in this case, Hudson).

Although I haven't said it explicitly, the requirement that you must build iOS apps on Mac hardware means that your build automation tool must be able to deal with Mac OS X. In the case of Hudson, this isn't an issue, since it's a pure Java tool. Other proprietary tools may work with Macs, or may have client plug-ins that let your remotely run a build on a Mac. If your tool can't communicate with a Mac in any way, you're kinda out of luck, and may have to sell your build automation group on letting you use a tool such as Hudson instead.

All the tools in this section require Java. Java used to be installed as part of the Mac OS X install, but starting with Lion, it needs to be installed explicitly, you can download the latest version of Java for Lion from Apple.

Begin by downloading Hudson from *http://hudson-ci.org/*. They have native packages for Linux systems but not, alas, MacOS. What they have is a WAR file, which is a Java Web Application Archive, meant to be dropped into a Java web server such as Tomcat. Tomcat doesn't have an installer for Mac OS X either, so you need to download the "core" Tomcat zip file from *http://tomcat.apache.org/*. You can probably download the most recent shipping version safely, but if in doubt, the Hudson site should list the compatible versions of Tomcat.

Once you've unzipped the Tomcat archive, you should end up with a directory hierarchy that looks something like this:

```
tomcat
    --> bin
    --> conf
    --> lib
    --> logs
    --> temp
    --> webapps
    --> work
```

Place the Hudson WAR file in the Tomcat *webapps* directory, and then change directories to the Tomcat *bin* directory, and run *startup.sh*. You should see terminal output that looks like this:

```
~Tom Tom$ cd ./tomcat/bin
bin Tom$ ./startup.sh
Using CATALINA_BASE:   /Volumes/Homes/Tom/tomcat
Using CATALINA_HOME:   /Volumes/Homes/Tom/tomcat
Using CATALINA_TMPDIR: /Volumes/Homes/Tom/tomcat/temp
Using JRE_HOME:   /System/Library/Frameworks/JavaVM.framework/Versions/CurrentJDK/Home
Using CLASSPATH:       /Volumes/Homes/Tom/tomcat/bin/bootstrap.jar
```

Give Tomcat and Hudson a few minutes to start up, and then you should be able to browse to *http://localhost:8080/hudson*, and get a screen resembling the one in Figure 3-1.

Again, an entire book could be written about the many ways you can customize Hudson, so it won't be covered in any detail here. For example, you can set up users and permissions, have Tomcat (and thus Hudson) start automatically when the Mac boots, and much more. For the scope of this book, we're going to focus on creating a Hudson job to build our application automatically.

Figure 3-1. The Hudson screen on first time startup

Creating the Build Job

For the remainder of this chapter, we're going to assume that you have an Xcode project checked into a source control system, as outlined in the last chapter. Since the entire point of automating your builds is to take the most recent version of your project under source control and create a build of the app from it, it is obviously a prerequisite.

I've set up a repository on github that has all the examples in this book, as well as the tools and utilities mentioned. You can check a read-only copy out of git by using the repository URL:

git://github.com/blackbear/enterprise-ios-applications.git

With Hudson up and running, we can start implementing our automated build. Helpfully, Hudson places a link to what we want to do right at the upper left hand corner, *New Job*. If you click on that link, you're brought to an intermediate page that asks you to name your job, and select what type of build it is (see Figure 3-2). For the purposes of this walk-through, we won't look into these options in detail, just give the build a name (BuggyWhipBuild) and set it up as a freestyle project.

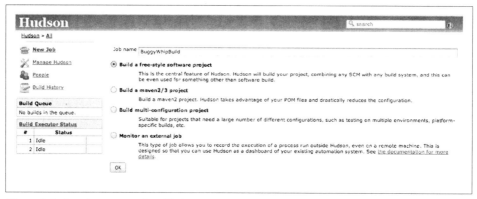

Figure 3-2. Creating a new job in Hudson

The Main Configuration Screen

Once that page is submitted, you're brought to a longer page where you will configure the build (Figure 3-3). Especially when you are first starting out with Hudson, it is a good idea to take things step by step, rather than try to get it all working at once, so that's the approach we'll take. The first section of the configuration has four check-boxes, which we can discuss briefly.

Discard old builds

If you leave this box unchecked, Hudson will keep every build ever made until you run out of disk space. Usually, you only want a few builds available (perhaps as many as a month's worth, but probably not more). By checking this box, you will be given the option to select the number of days back or number of builds to keep. You can also choose (using the advanced checkbox) to select a different number of days to keep artifacts (the finished output products) of builds, which in the case of an iOS build would be things such as test results and IPA files.

This build is parameterized

This is an option you will almost never use with automated builds, because it will cause the build to prompt the user for parameters that will be passed into the build process. Obviously, this isn't practical for builds designed to run unattended.

Disable build

This item is self-explanatory. If it is checked, scheduled builds will not occur.

Figure 3-3. The main build configuration screen

Execute concurrent builds

Again, not an option you are likely to need—it allows Hudson to run multiple builds simultaneously, if the resources have been configured to allow for it. If you wish to do it, there shouldn't be an issue doing this with Xcode builds.

Advanced options

In general, a stand-alone iOS build project should not need to set these options. They deal with cross-build dependencies, how often to retry failed builds, and what directory to perform the build in. You can ignore them for the moment.

Source Code Management with Hudson

The next section of the configuration screen deals with source code management. Specifically, it deals with how to check out the project so that a build can be performed on it. On the Hudson website, there is a long list of SCM systems that can be integrated into Hudson using plug-ins, including git, Mercurial, Visual SourceSafe, MKS, and many others. For the purposes of this example, we'll stick with our existing CVS project that we used in the previous chapter. If you click on the CVS radio button, a new section expands out (Figure 3-4).

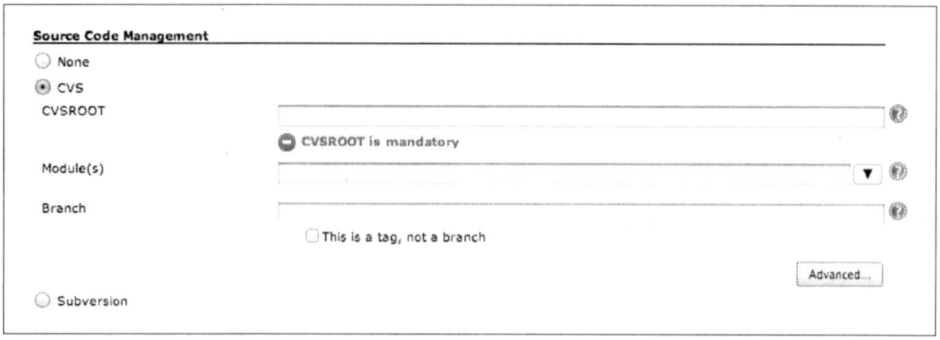

Source Code Management

○ None

◉ CVS

CVSROOT

🔴 CVSROOT is mandatory

Module(s)

Branch

☐ This is a tag, not a branch

Advanced…

○ Subversion

Figure 3-4. Configuring CVS in Hudson

To make this work, all we need to do is set the CVSROOT to the appropriate directory, the module to the module name of our project (BuggyWhipChat), and optionally decide which branch we wish to check out (if none is provided, the main trunk is checked out for CVS).

Obviously, depending on which source control system you use, you will end up providing different parameters to this section, but the idea remains the same: you will end up with a copy of your Xcode project checked out and ready to be built.

Before we go any further, let's make sure that the piece we've done so far is working correctly. With the SCM section filled out, you have enough done to try running the project. At the bottom of the page, press the *Save* button, which will return you to a view of your build (Figure 3-5).

Figure 3-5. The initially configured iOS build

Trying Your First Build

To try out the build, all you need to do is click on the *Build Now* link in the left-hand side list of links, A progress bar will appear under the Build History heading, and a few seconds later, the build will be complete and a link to the finished build will appear in the history. If you click on the link, and then click on *Console Output* link on the next page, you can see what happened under the covers.

```
Started by user anonymous
[BuggyWhipBuild] $ cvs -Q -zO -d /usr/local/CVS co -P \
    -d workspace -D "Monday, July 11, 2011 12:40:39 AM UTC" buggywhipchat
$ no changes detected
Finished: SUCCESS
```

Since all the job did was to check the sources out of CVS, there wasn't much excitement to be seen. If you look in your home directory, you will see a hidden directory called *.hudson*. Walking down the directories to *.hudson/jobs/BuggyWhipBuild/workspace*, you'll see a copy of your project checked out and waiting for you to build it. So now we're set to actually start playing with Xcode and making some apps!

Creating an Ant Build File

As has been previously mentioned, Hudson prefers to use Ant as the build tool to build projects. That's not to say that this is your only choice: you could almost as easily use GnuMake or any other tool that can be executed from the command line. But really, there's no reason not to use Ant, unless you're violently opposed to it for some reason. As opposed to gmake, which tends to be finicky on random characters in the file and can be a bit arcane to understand, Ant uses XML files that can be edited and validated in any standard XML editor. It will also make all your Java friends happy, because Ant is the build tool of choice for Java.

Ant build files can get quite complex, but they don't need to. All you really need is a single file called *build.xml*, and that's the file we're about to create. Example 3-1 shows a very simple build.xml file that does absolutely nothing.

Example 3-1. A simple build file

```
<?xml version="1.0" encoding="utf-8"?>
<project name="Buggy Whip Builder" default="debugbuild" basedir=".">
    <target name="debugbuild">
        <echo message="Debug Build Will Go Here"/>
    </target>
</project>
```

Let's break the file down line by line. The first line is a standard XML header. The next line, which uses the project tag, defines the name of the project that is associated with this build file, the default target (`debugbuild`) that the file builds if given no arguments, and the base directory that all commands will be executed relative to.

With this file placed in the root of the CVS project (which, you may remember, has the BuggyWhipChat and ChatAPI directories as subdirectories), we can run Ant from the command line and see the build script work:

```
tom Tom:buggywhipchat$ ant
Buildfile: /Volumes/Homes/Tom/buggwhipchat/build.xml

debugbuild:
    [echo] Debug Build Will Go Here

BUILD SUCCESSFUL
Total time: 0 seconds
```

Testing xcodebuild

I know it seems like we've spent a lot of time discussing non-Xcode stuff, but now that we've assured ourselves that the basic Ant script is working, we can start to actually wire up Xcode to the build. Making command-line builds work comes down to understanding a few basic commands that are included in the developer SDK. The star of the show is *xcodebuild*, which you can find in the */Developer/usr/bin* directory. The basic format of the command is:

```
xcodebuild [-project projectname] [-target targetname] ...
[-configuration configurationname] [buildaction] ...
```

There is an alternate format that is used if you are dealing with workspaces:

```
xcodebuild [-workspace workspacename] [-scheme schemename] ...
[-configuration configurationname] [buildaction] ...
```

The major difference is that the workspace version replaces the project and target specifications with the more "modern" workspace and scheme ones.

Since we're working with a workspace-based project, we'll be using the second form of the command. Before trying to integrate it into our build system, we should make sure that we can run the command correctly, directly from the command line:

```
buggywhipchat Diane$ /Developer/usr/bin/xcodebuild -workspace \
  BuggyWhipChat.xcworkspace -scheme BuggyWhipChat build
=== BUILD NATIVE TARGET ChatAPI OF PROJECT ChatAPI WITH CONFIGURATION Debug ===
Check dependencies
.
.
.
=== BUILD NATIVE TARGET BuggyWhipChat OF PROJECT BuggyWhipChat WITH CONFIGURATION
Debug ===
Check dependencies
.
.
.
/usr/bin/codesign --force --sign "iPhone Developer: Diane Coder (UU7RPZZZZZ)"
** BUILD SUCCEEDED **
```

So, the first good news is that the build worked. But what exactly happened? We can start by looking at the command we executed. We specified the workspace we wanted to use (which is in the current directory, the same one that has the *build.xml* file in it. The scheme we asked for is the BuggyWhipChat scheme, which is the standard scheme that builds a debug build. Finally, we asked for a build action of build (which, by the way, is the default). We'll look at some of the other build actions later on—there are also a number of other arguments that you can pass to *xcodebuild* that will allow you to tweak the build settings that you normally set via the Xcode project inspector. If you're interested, running *man xcodebuild* from the command line will give you the information in detail.

Integrating xcodebuild into an Ant Script

The next step is to take the *xcodebuild* command that worked so well on the command line, and make it work from inside Ant. The key to this is the *exec* task of Ant, which lets you fire off any command line you desire from inside Ant. In our case, we're going to modify our *build.xml* to look like Example 3-2.

Example 3-2. build.xml with the xcodebuild

```xml
<?xml version="1.0" encoding="utf-8"?>
<project name="Buggy Whip Builder" default="debugbuild" basedir=".">
   <target name="debugbuild">
      <echo message="Building debug build of BuggyWhipChat"/>
      <exec executable="/Developer/usr/bin/xcodebuild" os="Mac OS X">
         <arg value="-workspace"/>
         <arg value="BuggyWhipChat.xcworkspace"/>
         <arg value="-scheme"/>
         <arg value="BuggyWhipChat"/>
         <arg value="build"/>
      </exec>
   </target>
</project>
```

This is fairly straightforward: we've added an exec task that runs the *xcodebuild* command, passing in the arguments that we've already determined will work. The os parameter of the *exec* task ensures that we don't try to run this script on a non-Mac, but to be thorough, we should really use an *if* task and print an error message if the we're not on a Mac. With this in place, we can try running Ant from the command line, and see what we get:

```
buggywhipchat Diane$ ant
Buildfile: /Volumes/Homes/James/Dropbox/Dianescvs/buggywhipchat/build.xml

debugbuild:
     [echo] Building debug build of BuggyWhipChat
    [exec] === BUILD NATIVE TARGET ChatAPI OF PROJECT ChatAPI WITH CONFIGURATION Debug ===
  .
  .
```

```
[exec]
[exec] ** BUILD SUCCEEDED **
[exec]
```

Houston, we have a build! But we're not quite done yet.

Calling the Ant Script from Hudson

The whole purpose of this exercise was to get our builds hooked up into Hudson. Now that we have a good Ant script, we can tell Hudson to use it. But before we forget, we need to add the build script to our CVS repository.

```
buggywhipchat Diane$ cvs add build.xml
cvs add: scheduling file `build.xml' for addition
cvs add: use `cvs commit' to add this file permanently
buggywhipchat Diane$ cvs commit
```

Now we can go back to our Hudson configuration, and make a few changes. To begin, let's make sure that we start with an empty directory before we check our project out from CVS, you do this by making sure that the "Use Update" option in the advanced portion of the Source Control Management section of the configuration is turned off, as shown in Figure 3-6. This will cause Hudson to start with a clean slate every time, which can be especially important if you end up with work products in your build directory. This also saves you the hassle of having to run an *xcodebuild* clean action before doing your build.

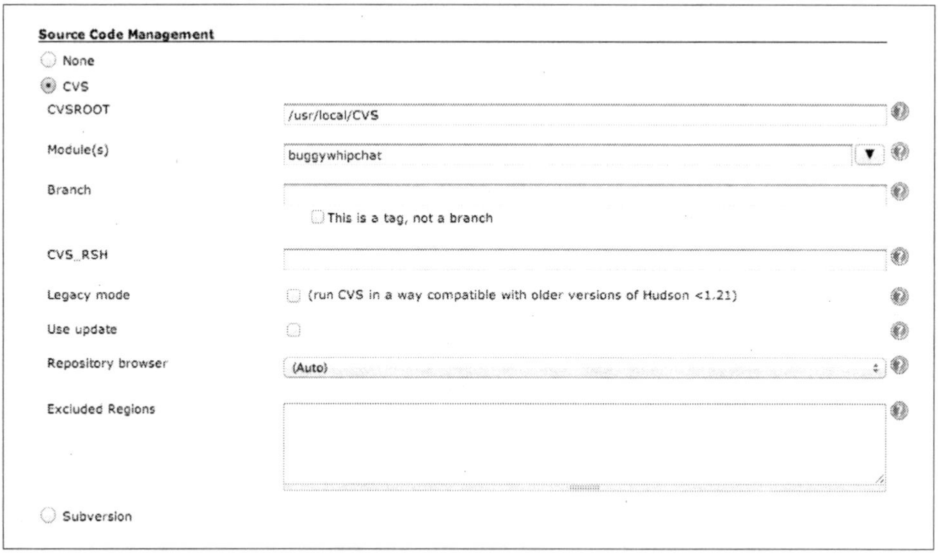

Figure 3-6. Turning off the Use Update flag

The other step required is to add a build step, which is done by going down to the Build section of the configuration, and clicking on the Add Build Step pulldown (Figure 3-7). From this menu, we want to use Invoke Ant.

Figure 3-7. Adding an Ant task to Hudson

Selecting this choice gives use a single parameter to fill out: the targets to build. In this case, we want to use the *debugbuild* target, so we fill that in (Figure 3-8) and save the configuration. Now we're ready to rumble!

Figure 3-8. Setting up the Ant target

If we go back to the main Hudson window and hit the play button for the build, which tells Hudson to start running the build, we should (if everything went according to plan) end up with a good build. Going into the new build, we can look at the console output, and see everything worked as expected:

```
Started by user anonymous
[BuggyWhipBuild] $ cvs -Q -z0 -d /usr/local/CVS co -P \
  -d workspace -D "Friday, July 15, 2011 3:41:38 PM UTC" buggywhipchat
$ computing changelog
[workspace] $ ant debugbuild
Buildfile: /Volumes/Homes/James/.hudson/jobs/BuggyWhipBuild/workspace/build.xml
debugbuild:
    [echo] Building debug build of BuggyWhipChat
    [exec] === BUILD NATIVE TARGET ChatAPI OF PROJECT ChatAPI WITH CONFIGURATION Debug
===
   .
   .
```

```
     [exec] ** BUILD SUCCEEDED **
     [exec] BUILD SUCCESSFUL
Total time: 12 seconds
Finished: SUCCESS
```

Getting Fancy with Hudson

Now that we have the basic build running, there are a few things we can do within Hudson and our project to make life easier for us later on.

Running a Nightly Build

The first one is fairly simple—we can set the build to run automatically every night, to make sure that we have a good nightly build. To do this, go back into the configuration screen for the build in Hudson, and scroll down to the section entitled Build Triggers. In there, you'll see a checkbox called "Build periodically," and if you check it, you'll get an empty Schedule field you can type in (Figure 3-9). This is essentially the build's personal cron file, and follows pretty much the same format. If you've never used cron, you can click on the ? icon, and a tutorial will appear below the field. So to run a build every night at 2:05 AM, you'd enter:

```
5 2 * * *
```

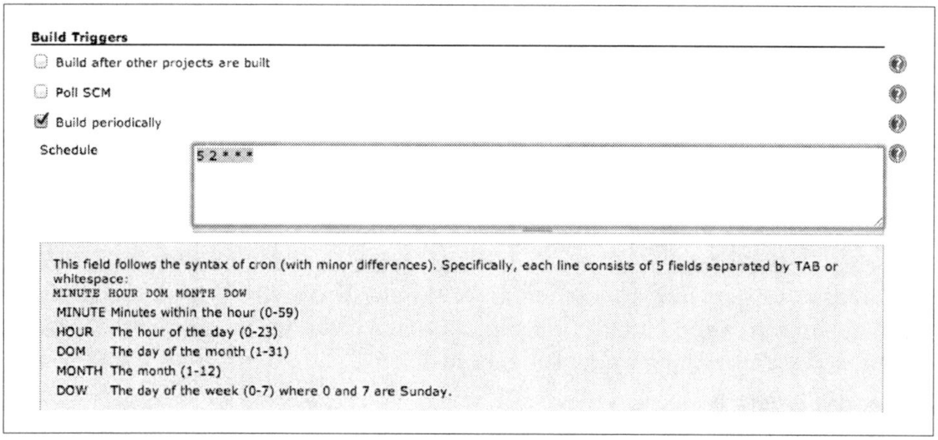

Figure 3-9. Configuring a build to run nightly

Now (assuming that Hudson is up and running at the time), you'll get a nightly build. If you're feeling ambitious, you can configure the build to send you status messages via email (and even set it not to bother you unless the build fails!).

In Chapter 7, we'll go one step further, and actually use TestFlight to send new builds directly to our testers.

Include the Build Number Directly into the Application Version

Eventually, you're going to get a bug report, and after spending hours trying to reproduce it, you may learn that the user was running an old build. Grrrrr! Wouldn't it be great if we could automatically bump up the minor version number of the application every time we did a build? Well, Bunky, you're in luck! It turns out that with a few magic steps, you can do just that.

The first step is the simplest of all, you just need to put a string in your version number (and short version number) in your *applicationname-info.plist* file, something unlikely to occur anywhere else in the file. I like to use BUILDNUM in all caps. So, if your version number for your application is 1.0, you'd use `1.0.BUILDNUM` as the version number for the two properties in the plist (see Figure 3-10).

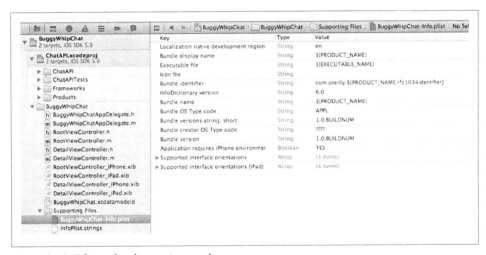

Figure 3-10. Editing the plist version number

There's only one more step we need to take here, which is to tell Hudson to run a small shell script, which will replace the `BUILDNUM` string with the actual build number (which, helpfully, Hudson exposes as an environment variable to shell scripts it runs).

Go back into the configuration for our build, and create a new build step (in the same way that we created the Ant build step earlier). But, this time, rather than selecting Invoke Ant, select Execute Shell. You'll end up with a text box directly beneath the existing Ant target text box. Before we do anything else, grab the step by the little grey box "handle" on the left, and drag it above the Ant step, because we want to edit the plist entries before the build runs.

The script itself is trivial, and is shown in Example 3-3.

Example 3-3. A perl script to set the build number in the version string

```
cd BuggyWhipChat/BuggyWhipChat
/usr/bin/perl -p -i -e "s/BUILDNUM/$BUILD_NUMBER/g" BuggyWhipChat-Info.plist
```

So what's going on here? First, we move ourselves to the right directory with *cd*, in this case the subdirectory that contains the plist file we want to modify. Then we use a perl "in-place" edit to substitute the string BUILDNUM for the BUILD_NUMBER environment variable globally in the file. Since this step occurs before *xcodebuild* is run, the version number in the binary will reflect the build number we set.

If we run the build again (after checking the modified plist file into CVS, of course), we can verify that the step ran by looking at the build console output, which will now contain this snippet:

```
$ computing changelog[workspace]
$ /bin/sh -xe /Volumes/Homes/Diane/tomcat/temp/hudson3475590830804804920.sh
+ cd BuggyWhipChat/BuggyWhipChat
+ /usr/bin/perl -p -i -e s/BUILDNUM/6/g BuggyWhipChat-Info.plist
```

In this case, BUILDNUM is being replaced by 6, the current build number. If we take a peek at the plist in the finished build workspace directory (which hides in *~/.hudson/jobs/ buildname/workspace/*), we can also see that the strings were appropriately modified in the actual file:

```
<key>CFBundleShortVersionString</key>
<string>1.0.6</string>
<key>CFBundleSignature</key>
<string>????</string>
<key>CFBundleVersion</key>
<string>1.0.6</string>
```

Parameterize the Build Script

As you go along, you're going to end up running a number of different Xcode builds as part of your automated build process. You'll be running unit-test-only builds, debug builds, Ad Hoc builds, and maybe even App Store builds. They all are the same, except for the scheme and action you specify to *xcodebuild*—so why not make a parameterized custom Ant task, and save some copy-and-paste scripting?

Go back into your *build.xml* file, and change it to look like Example 3-4.

Example 3-4. A parameterized build.xml file

```
<?xml version="1.0" encoding="utf-8"?>
<project name="Buggy Whip Builder" default="debugbuild" basedir=".">
   <macrodef name="xcodebuild">
      <attribute name="workspace"/>
      <attribute name="scheme"/>
      <attribute name="action" default="build"/>
      <sequential>
```

```
            <echo message="Running xcodebuild using workspace '@{workspace}',\
            scheme '@{scheme}', action '@{action}'"/>
            <exec executable="/Developer/usr/bin/xcodebuild" os="Mac OS X">
                <arg value="-workspace"/>
                <arg value="@{workspace}"/>
                <arg value="-scheme"/>
                <arg value="@{scheme}"/>
                <arg value="@{action}"/>
            </exec>
        </sequential>
    </macrodef>
    <target name="debugbuild">
        <xcodebuild workspace="BuggyWhipChat.xcworkspace" scheme="BuggyWhipChat"/>
    </target>
</project>
```

What we've done here is to create a macro called *xcodebuild* that takes three parameters, one of them with a default value if not supplied. Now, in the rest of our code, we can invoke an Xcode build using a single command, which supplies values for those parameters. We'll be using this handy macro through the rest of the book, and you'll see how much copy-and-paste it saves.

With our project building automatically and inserting build numbers into the version strings, it's time to actually do some coding. In the next chapter, we'll see how to get your iPhone application talking to a number of popular web service formats.

CHAPTER 4

Integrating iOS Applications into Enterprise Services

In the early days of software development, you ran your programs directly on a computer, sitting in front of the console. Later, the idea of timesharing and remote sessions came into being, bringing with it the rise of the 3270 and VT-100 terminals, along with punch cards and paper tape. Later, network computing became the rage, with Sun famously proclaiming that the network was the computer. We got RPC, CORBA, and we've evolved today into SOAP, REST, and AJAX. But no matter what it's called, or what format the data moves in, all these technologies attempt to solve the same problem, the same one that has existed since client-server architectures first came upon the earth.

As an iOS developer, you face the same problem today. You need to be able to reliably and (hopefully) easily integrate user-facing UI with all the messy business logic, persistence, security, and magic unicorn blood that does all the hard work on the backend.*

The Rules of the Road

There are basically two possible scenarios when integrating iOS applications into Enterprise services. Either you are starting from scratch on both ends, or you have some legacy service with which you need to ingratiate your new application. The former situation is vastly preferable, because you can fine-tune your protocols and payloads to the demands of mobile clients, but the later scenario is probably the more likely one. In any event, I'll talk in general about each of them, and then look at some specific techniques for dealing with various protocols and payloads under iOS.

---

* Note: Magic Unicorn Blood contains chemicals known to the state of California to cause cancer, birth defects, or other reproductive harm. Please consider the use of Magic Pixie Dust in place of Magic Unicorn Blood when feasible.

Rule 1: Insist on Contract-Driven Development

Modern IDEs and service toolkits can take a lot of the grunt work out of creating service interfaces. They can auto-generate classes for you, create testing frameworks, generate documentation, and I wouldn't be surprised if they could prepare world-class sushi on demand by now. But there's one thing that they can do that is the bane of every client developer on the planet, and that's to auto-generate the interface from the backing classes. Java-based SOAP development is getting to be semi-notorious for this. On paper, it's great. Just sprinkle magic annotations in your source code, and tools such as CXF will figure it all out, generate the WSDL files, and you're good to go.

Unfortunately, in reality, you end up with a couple of problems. For one, you give up control over what the SOAP structures (or RESTful XML structures) are going to look like. I have seen some unforgivably butt-ugly XML produced by class-driven interface development. But more seriously, it means that "innocent" changes made to the underlying Java classes can have unforeseen repercussions on the payload, causing mysterious failures. There's nothing like doing your first regression test against a new server release where "nothing changed," and finding out that the payloads have been fundamentally altered by a trivial change in the server-side classes.

Because of this, I consider it almost a necessity that both sides of the house adhere to a contract-first approach to APIs. TDD is great for this: you can write some SOAPUI tests to exercise the specified contract, which will fail until the service is implemented. This keeps the server-side developers honest, because the acceptance test for their service is whether or not it passes the SOAPUI tests, and later on down the road, it will make sure they don't break the API contract.

Rule 2: Be Neither Chunky Nor Chatty

A friend of mine, web services guru Anne Thomas Manes of Burton Group, likes to say that web services should be chunky, not chatty. That is to say, it's better to send down too much information in a single request, rather than make dozens of calls to get the data, paying the latency toll on each request.

In general, I agree with her, especially since in a 3G (or worse) mobile environment, the latency can get quite painful. But on mobile devices, keeping down the payload size can be just as important. Not only do many users pay by the byte, but you have much more restrictive memory profiles on mobile devices. Thankfully, this isn't as much of a factor on an iOS device, because there tends to be plenty of memory available to the foreground process, but on Android or J2ME devices, available memory can be quite limited. If you suck down a 4MB XML payload as a string, and then parse it into an XML DOM, you could have 8MB of memory being consumed just by the data.

Of course, if you're only developing the protocol for iOS consumption, you only need to worry about bankrupting your users when they get their data plan bill, but these days, no one develops backend services for a single mobile platform, so you may have to live with constraints imposed by the needs of lesser devices. In a perfect world, try to design your protocols to allow for both chunky and chatty requests, and let the client decide how much data they want to consume at once.

First Things First: Getting a Connection

I'm going to make a general assumption for the body of this chapter, which is that whatever you are talking to, you're doing it via HTTP (or HTTPS). If you're doing something custom using sockets, the 1990s are calling and they would like their architecture back. In all seriousness, though, almost all client-server mobile work these days is done using HTTP for transport.[†]

The iOS SDK comes with a perfectly adequate HTTP implementation, found in the CFNetwork framework. But anyone who uses it is a masochist, because it makes you do so much of the work yourself. Until recently, I would have recommended using the ASIHttpRequest package. ASI stands for All Seeing Interactive (or "eye"), by the way, so if you happen to be an Illuminati conspiracist, this may not be the software for you. Why did I like this package so much?

It is licensed under the über-flexible BSD license, so you can do pretty much anything you want with it, and it provides a lot of the messy housekeeping code that HTTP requests tend to involve. Specifically, it will automatically handle:

> Easy access to request and response headers
> Authentication support
> Cookie support
> GZIP payload support
> Background request handling in iOS 4 and later
> Persistent connections
> Synchronous and asynchronous requests
> (And more!)

However, after the early access version of this book was released, I learned that ASIHttpRequest is in danger of becoming an orphan project. This is especially disturbing, because it means it may never be converted over to ARC, among other things. It would be more disturbing if it were the only game in town; until recently, it was, because the system-provided alternative, NSURLConnection, didn't support asynchronous requests. Being able to choose synchronous and asynchronous requests is critically important. Almost all of the time, you want to use asynchronous requests, even if the request *seems* synchronous. For example, a login may seem synchronous. After all, you can't really do anything further until the request completes. But in reality, if you do a real synchronous HTTP request, everything locks up (including activity

---

[†] Yes, I know, technically HTTP is the Application Layer, according to the OSI model. My apologies to pedantic taxonomists.

indicators) until the response returns. The pattern you want to use is to lock the UI (typically by setting various UI elements to have userInteractionEnabled set false), and then make an asynchronous call with both the success and failure callbacks re-enabling the UI.

Thankfully, in iOS 5, the system-provided class was extended to include asynchronous requests, so there's no longer a reason to avoid using it.

Using NSURLConnection—The BuggyWhip News Network

Let's see this package put through its paces, in this case by creating a page in the BuggyWhipChat application that lets you see the latest news on buggy whips. Unfortunately, the server folks haven't gotten the news feed working yet, so we'll be using CNN for testing. The page itself is going to be simple, a new button on the iPad toolbar that gets the CNN home page, and displays the HTML in an alert. Yes, this is a totally useless example, but we are talking about BuggyWhipCo here! Actually, the reason that we're not doing more with the HTML is two-fold: there's a perfectly good UIWeb View control that already does this, and the point is to highlight the NSURLConnection package, not to display web pages.

First, we add the toolbar item to the detail XIB and hook it up the "Sent Action" for the button to a new IBAction called showNews in the view controller, as shown in Example 4-1.

Example 4-1. A simple example using NSURLConnection

```
- (void)handleError:(NSString *)error{
    UIAlertView *alert =
            [[UIAlertView alloc]
            initWithTitle:@"Buggy Whip News Error"
            message: error
            delegate:self cancelButtonTitle:@"OK"
            otherButtonTitles:nil, nil];
    [alert show];
}

-(IBAction) showNews:(id) sender {
    NSURL *url = [NSURL URLWithString:@"http://www.cnn.com/index.html"];
    NSURLRequest *request = [NSURLRequest requestWithURL:url];
    [NSURLConnection
        sendAsynchronousRequest:request
        queue:[NSOperationQueue currentQueue]
        completionHandler:^(NSURLResponse *response,
                            NSData *data, NSError *error) {
            if (error != nil) {
                [self handleError:[error localizedDescription]];
            } else {
                [self displayResponse:data];
                if ([response isKindOfClass:[NSHTTPURLResponse class]]) {
                    NSHTTPURLResponse *httpresp =
```

```
            (NSHTTPURLResponse *) response;
            if ([httpresp statusCode] == 404) {
                [self handleError:@"Page not found!"];
            } else {
                [self displayResponse:data];
            }
        }
    }
  }];
}
```

So, what's going on here? Most of the action takes place in the showNews method, which is triggered by the button push of the new tab bar item. When it is pressed, the code creates an NSURL reference to the CNN website, and then creates an NSURLRequest HttpRequest instance using the requestWithURL method. There are a number of parameters you can set on the returned object, some of which I cover later, but by default, you get an HTTP GET request. Next, we use the sendAsynchronousRequest method of the NSURLConnection class to actually perform the request. This method is handed three parameters: the request we just created, the NSOperationQueue to run the request on (which, for thread safety, will usually be the current queue), and a block which serves as the completion handler (that is, the handler that deals with successful or failed calls).

If the request fails catastrophically (connection failures, server failures, etc.), the failure is returned in the error parameter, which will be non-null. If the call succeeds, which can include 401 (unauthorized) and 404 (not found) errors, the call response is populated along with the body of the response as an NSData object. You can proceed to process the response body, returned in the data parameter.

If we run the application and click on the tab bar button, we get the expected results, shown in Figure 4-1.

If we change the hardwired string that we use to create the URL to something bogus, such as *http://www.cnnbuggywhip.com*, we get an alert message with the error shown in Figure 4-2.

But suppose we specify a valid host name, but an invalid address, such as http://www.cnn.com/buggywhipco.html? As I mentioned, a 404 error is considered a success and will call the success selector, leading to something like the alert in Figure 4-3.

What we really want to have happen here is to display a meaningful alert message, something that we could internationalize, for example. So, we need to look a bit more carefully at allegedly "good" responses, leading to the rewritten method shown in Example 4-2.

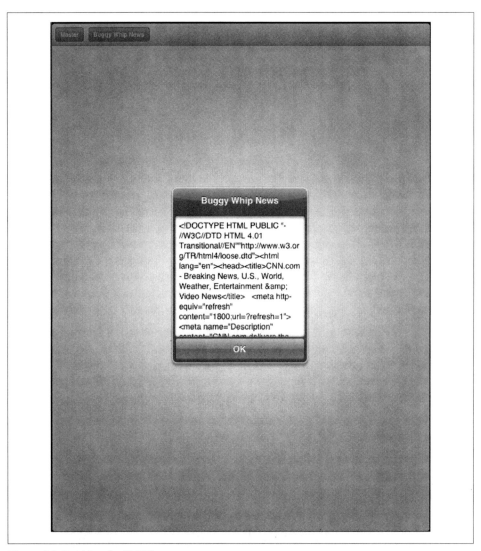

Figure 4-1. Fetching the CNN home page

Figure 4-2. The response to a bogus URL

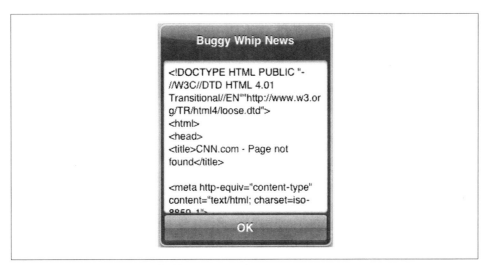

Figure 4-3. Connecting to a bad address on a good server

Example 4-2. A more robust success method

```
-(IBAction) showNews:(id) sender {
    NSURL *url = [NSURL URLWithString:@"http://www.cnn.com/index.html"];
    NSURLRequest *request = [NSURLRequest requestWithURL:url];
    [NSURLConnection
      sendAsynchronousRequest:request
      queue:[NSOperationQueue currentQueue]
      completionHandler:^(NSURLResponse *response,
                          NSData *data, NSError *error) {
        if (error != nil) {
            [self handleError:[error localizedDescription]];
        } else {
            if ([response isKindOfClass:[NSHTTPURLResponse class]]) {
                NSHTTPURLResponse *httpresp =
                  (NSHTTPURLResponse *) response;
                if ([httpresp statusCode] == 404) {
                    [self handleError:@"Page not found!"];
                } else {
                    [self displayResponse:data];
                }
            }
        }
    }];
}
```

What has happened here is that we have checked to see that the response is really an NSHTTPURLResponse object (which it should be for any HTTP request). If so, you can cast the response object to that type, and use the statusCode method to check that you haven't gotten a 404, 401, or other HTTP protocol error.

Something a Little More Practical—Parsing XML Response

Now that we've had a brief introduction to using `NSURLRequest`, we can use it to do something a bit more useful than spitting out raw HTML in alerts. We still don't have any web services from the backend developers, so we'll use a publicly available RESTful web service provided by the US National Weather Service. Given an address such as:
http://www.weather.gov/forecasts/xml/sample_products/browser_interface/
ndfdXMLclient.php?zipCodeList=20910+25414&product=time-series&begin=2004
-01-01T00:00:00&end=2013-04-21T00:00:00&maxt=maxt&mint=mint

We can get back XML that looks like the sample shown in Example 4-3.

Example 4-3. Sample XML from the National Weather Service

```
<dwml xmlns:xsd="http://www.w3.org/2001/XMLSchema"
    xmlns:xsi="http://www.w3.org/2001/XMLSchema-instance"
    version="1.0"
    xsi:noNamespaceSchemaLocation=\
    "http://www.nws.noaa.gov/forecasts/xml/DWMLgen/\
    schemaDWML.xsd">
  <head>
    <product srsName="WGS 1984"
             concise-name="time-series"
             operational-mode="official">
      <title>
        NOAA's National Weather Service Forecast Data
      </title>
      <field>meteorological</field>
      <category>forecast</category>
      <creation-date refresh-frequency="PT1H">
             2011-07-25T00:30:56Z
      </creation-date>
    </product>
    <source>
      <more-information>
        http://www.nws.noaa.gov/forecasts/xml/
      </more-information>
      <production-center>
        Meteorological Development Laboratory
        <sub-center>
          Product Generation Branch
        </sub-center>
      </production-center>
      <disclaimer>
          http://www.nws.noaa.gov/disclaimer.html
      </disclaimer>
      <credit>
          http://www.weather.gov/
      </credit>
      <credit-logo>
           http://www.weather.gov/images/xml_logo.gif
      </credit-logo>
```

```xml
        <feedback>
            http://www.weather.gov/feedback.php
        </feedback>
    </source>
</head>
<data>
    <location>
        <location-key>point1</location-key>
        <point latitude="42.90" longitude="-71.29"/>
    </location>
    <moreWeatherInformation applicable-location="point1">
        http://forecast.weather.gov/MapClick.php?\
        textField1=42.90&textField2=-71.29
    </moreWeatherInformation>
    <time-layout time-coordinate="local"
        summarization="none">
        <layout-key>k-p24h-n1-1</layout-key>
        <start-valid-time>
            2011-07-26T08:00:00-04:00
        </start-valid-time>
        <end-valid-time>
            2011-07-26T20:00:00-04:00
        </end-valid-time>
    </time-layout>
    <time-layout time-coordinate="local"
        summarization="none">
        <layout-key>k-p24h-n1-2</layout-key>
        <start-valid-time>
            2011-07-26T20:00:00-04:00
        </start-valid-time>
        <end-valid-time>
            2011-07-27T09:00:00-04:00
        </end-valid-time>
    </time-layout>
    <parameters applicable-location="point1">
        <temperature type="maximum"
            units="Fahrenheit" time-layout="k-p24h-n1-1">
            <name>Daily Maximum Temperature</name>
            <value>82</value>
        </temperature>
        <temperature type="minimum"
            units="Fahrenheit" time-layout="k-p24h-n1-2">
            <name>Daily Minimum Temperature</name>
            <value>61</value>
        </temperature>
    </parameters>
</data>
</dwml>
```

There's a mouthful of data in that payload, but essentially, given a zip code and a start
and end date, the service will return a list of high and low temperature forecasts that
lie between those dates. Let's use this service to create a more interesting alert.

We can start by writing a utility function to generate the correct endpoint for the REST request, given a series of parameters. By creating a stand-alone generator, it will be easier to unit test that logic. So, we create a `WebServiceEndpointGenerator` class, with a static method to create the appropriate endpoint, which looks like Example 4-4.

Example 4-4. A web service endpoint generator

```
+(NSURL *) getForecastWebServiceEndpoint:(NSString *) zipcode startDate:(NSDate *)
    startDate endDate:(NSDate *) endDate {
    NSDateFormatter *df = [NSDateFormatter new];
    [df setDateFormat:@"YYYY-MM-dd'T'hh:mm:ss"];
    NSString *url =
        [NSString stringWithFormat:
            @"http://www.weather.gov/forecasts/xml/\
            sample_products/browser_interface/\
            ndfdXMLclient.php?zipCodeList=%@\
            &product=time-series&begin=%@\
            &end=%@&maxt=maxt&mint=mint",
        zipcode, [df stringFromDate:startDate],
        [df stringFromDate:endDate]];
    [df release];
    return [NSURL URLWithString:url];
}
```

Back on our detail page, we add another bar button hooked up to a new selector, called `showWeather`. To save some space here, and because we're interested in the backend code, not the UI treatment, we'll have the success method for this call simply send the output to the log using `NSLog`. But how to extract the useful data? We could use string functions to find the pieces of the XML we were interested in, but that's laborious and not very robust. We could use the XML pull parser that comes with iOS, but pull parsers are also a bit of a pain, and I tend to avoid using them unless I need to significantly parse down the in-memory footprint of the data. So, since iOS doesn't have a native DOM parser, we'll dig one out of the open source treasure chest.

You actually have your choice of packages, TouchXML and KissXML. I prefer KissXML, because it can both parse XML to a DOM, and generate XML from a DOM, whereas TouchXML can only parse. KissXML is available at: *http://code.google.com/p/kissxml*. Integration largely involves copying files into the project, adding the libxml2 library, and one additional step: adding a directory to the include search path. The KissXML Wiki has all the details on how to add the package to your project.

I'll note here that KissXML is, at the moment, not compatible with the ARC compiler. For that reason, I highly recommend making it into a static library that you include in your main application, as described in Chapter 2.

With the library in place, we can use XPath to pluck just the data we want out of the returned payload from the web service; the code is shown in Example 4-5.

Example 4-5. Parsing XML with KissXML

```
-(id) getSingleStringValue:(DDXMLElement *) element xpath:(NSString *) xpath {
    NSError *error = nil;
    NSArray *vals = [element nodesForXPath:xpath error:&error];
    if (error != nil) {
        return nil;
    }
    if ([vals count] != 1) {
        return nil;
    }
    DDXMLElement *val = [vals objectAtIndex:0];
    return [val stringValue];
}


- (void)gotWeather:(NSData *)data
{
    UIAlertView *alert;
    NSError *error = nil;
    DDXMLDocument *ddDoc = [[DDXMLDocument alloc]
                            initWithXMLString:[[NSString alloc]
                                               initWithData:data
                                               encoding:NSUTF8StringEncoding]
                            options:0 error:&error];
    if (error == nil) {
        NSArray *timelayouts =
        [ddDoc nodesForXPath:@"//data/time-layout" error:&error];
        NSMutableDictionary *timeDict =
        [NSMutableDictionary new];
        for (DDXMLElement *timenode in timelayouts) {
            NSString *key =
            [self getSingleStringValue:timenode
                                xpath:@"layout-key"];
            if (key != nil) {
                NSArray *dates =
                [timenode nodesForXPath:@"start-valid-time" error:&error];
                NSMutableArray *dateArray = [NSMutableArray new];
                for (DDXMLElement *date in dates) {
                    [dateArray addObject:[date stringValue]];
                }
                [timeDict setObject:dateArray forKey:key];
            }
        }
        NSArray *temps =
        [ddDoc nodesForXPath:@"//parameters/temperature" error:&error];
        for (DDXMLElement *tempnode in temps) {
            NSString *type = [self getSingleStringValue:tempnode
                                                 xpath:@"@type"];
            NSString *units = [self getSingleStringValue:tempnode
                                                  xpath:@"@units"];
            NSString *timeLayout = [self getSingleStringValue:tempnode
                                                       xpath:@"@time-layout"];
            NSString *name = [self getSingleStringValue:tempnode xpath:@"name"];
            NSArray *values = [tempnode nodesForXPath:@"value" error:&error];
            int i = 0;
```

```
            NSArray *times = [timeDict valueForKey:timeLayout];
            for (DDXMLElement *value in values) {
                NSString *val = [value stringValue];
                NSLog(@"Type: %@, Units: %@, Time: %@",
                        type, units, [times objectAtIndex:i]);
                NSLog(@"Name: %@, Value: %@",
                        name, val);
                NSLog(@" ");
                i++;
            }
        }
        return;
    }
    alert = [[UIAlertView alloc] initWithTitle:@"Error parsing XML"
                                        message: [error localizedDescription]
                                        delegate:self
                            cancelButtonTitle:@"OK" otherButtonTitles:nil, nil];
    [alert show];
}

- (IBAction)showWeather:(id)sender {
    NSURL *url =
    [WebServiceEndpointGenerator
      getForecastWebServiceEndpoint:@"03038"
      startDate:[NSDate date]
      endDate:[[NSDate date]
            dateByAddingTimeInterval:3600*24*2]];
    NSURLRequest *request = [NSURLRequest requestWithURL:url];
    [NSURLConnection
      sendAsynchronousRequest:request
      queue:[NSOperationQueue currentQueue]
      completionHandler:^(NSURLResponse *response,
                        NSData *data, NSError *error) {
        if (error != nil) {
            [self handleError:error.description];
        } else {
            [self gotWeather:data];
        }
    }];
}
```

Let's take a good look at what's going on here. First off, we have the new handler for the weather button we added to the tab bar, called showWeather. What this method does is to construct an endpoint using the generator we just created. It passes in the zip code for Derry, NH (my home sweet home), and start and end dates that correspond to now and 24 hours from now. Then it does an asynchronous request to that URL using the same completion handler mechanism that we used in the previous example.

One advantage that the NSURLConnection method has over my previous choice, ASI HttpRequest, is that it is purely block-driven for the handlers. This can be significant when you have multiple asynchronous requests in flight, because a block-based handler lets you tie the handler directly to the request, rather than using selectors to specify the delegates to handler the responses.

The interesting bit, from an XML parsing perspective, is what happens inside the gotWeather method when the request succeeds. After doing the normal checks for bad status codes, it uses the initWithXMLString method of the DDXMLDocument class to parse the returned string into an XML DOM structure. The method takes a pointer to an NSError object as an argument, and that is what you should check after the call to see if the parse was successful.

Assuming the parse succeeded, the next step is to use the nodesForXPath method on the returned XML document, specifying //data/time-layout as the XPath to look for. This method returns an array of DDXMLElement objects, or nil if nothing matched the XPath specified. The weather XML we get back follows a pattern I find particularly obnoxious in XML DTDs: it makes you match up data from one part of the payload with data from another part. In this case, the time-layout elements have to be matched up with the attributes in the temperature elements, so we iterate over the time-layout elements, building a dictionary of the layout names to the dates they represent.

I find when working with KissXML that I frequently want to get the string value of a child node that I know only has a single instance. So I usually write a helper method such as the getSingleStringValue method used in this example. Using it, I can snatch the keys and start dates, and populate the dictionary with them. This method is shown in Example 4-6.

Example 4-6. The getSingleStringValue method

```
-(id) getSingleStringValue:(DDXMLElement *) element
                    xpath:(NSString *) xpath {
    NSError *error = nil;
    NSArray *vals = [element nodesForXPath:xpath error:&error];
    if (error != nil) {
        return nil;
    }
    if ([vals count] != 1) {
        return nil;
    }
    DDXMLElement *val = [vals objectAtIndex:0];
    return [val stringValue];
}
```

Basically, the method takes the root element for the extraction, and a relative or absolute XPath expressing as a string. It gets the array of matching elements, makes sure there wasn't an error (such as an invalid XPath string), and if it gets back exactly one element in the array, returns it.

Once I have the dictionary, I iterate over the temperature data, grabbing attributes and element values as appropriate, then use the diction to find the time associated with the reading. Finally, I dump the data out to the log, resulting in this kind of output:

```
Type: maximum, Units: Fahrenheit
2011-11-16T07:00:00-05:00, Daily Maximum Temperature = 58

2011-11-17T07:00:00-05:00, Daily Maximum Temperature = 49

2011-11-18T07:00:00-05:00, Daily Maximum Temperature = 48

Type: minimum, Units: Fahrenheit
2011-11-16T19:00:00-05:00, Daily Minimum Temperature = 42

2011-11-17T19:00:00-05:00, Daily Minimum Temperature = 27
```

Generating XML for Submission to Services

Whereas you almost always want to use a parsed DOM to extract data from a service,
how you construct XML to send back to a server is more flexible. The particular web
service we used in the last example is GET-only, so we'll use a mythical service that
takes a POST for this one. Let's say that the server crew has finally gotten their act
together, and you can now post a news item by sending the following XML:

```
<newsitem postdate="2011-07-01" posttime="14:54">
    <subject>
        Buggy Whips Now Available in Brown
    </subject>
    <body>
        Buggy whips are the hottest thing around these
        days, and now they're available in a new
        designer color, caramel brown!
    </body>
</newsitem>
```

If you wanted to construct payloads that follow this format, and post them up to the
server, you could use the code snippet in Example 4-7.

Example 4-7. Constructing XML by formatting strings

```
-(NSString *) constructNewsItemXMLByFormatWithSubject:(NSString *)
    subject body:(NSString *) body
{
    NSDate *now = [NSDate date];
    NSDateFormatter *df = [NSDateFormatter new];
    [df setDateFormat:@"YYYY-MM-dd"];
    NSDateFormatter *tf = [NSDateFormatter new];
    [tf setDateFormat:@"hh:mm"];
    NSString *xml =
        [NSString stringWithFormat:@"<newsitem\
         postdate=\"%@\" posttime=\"%@\">\
         <subject>%@<subject><body>%@</body></newsitem>",
                        [df stringFromDate:now],
                        [tf stringFromDate:now],
                        subject, body];

    return xml;
```

```
}

- (IBAction)sendNews:(id)sender {
    NSLog(@"By Format: %@",
        [self constructNewsItemXMLByFormatWithSubject:
            @"This is a test subject"
            body:@"Buggy whips are cool, aren't they?"]);
}
```

If we hook the sendNews IBAction up to a new bar button item and run the app, we can see that perfectly reasonable XML is produced:

```
By Format: <newsitem postdate="2011-07-26" posttime="10:42"> \
<subject>This is a test subject<subject>\
<body>Buggy whips are cool, aren't they?</body></newsitem>
```

Let's compare this with the corresponding code, done using DOM construction techniques (Example 4-8).

Example 4-8. Constructing XML by building a DOM

```
#import "DDXMLElementAdditions.h"
.
.
.
-(NSString *) constructNewsItemXMLByDOMWithSubject:
    (NSString *) subject body:(NSString *) body {
    NSDate *now = [NSDate date];
    NSDateFormatter *df = [NSDateFormatter new];
    [df setDateFormat:@"YYYY-MM-dd"];
    NSDateFormatter *tf = [NSDateFormatter new];
    [tf setDateFormat:@"hh:mm"];
    DDXMLElement *postdate =
        [DDXMLElement attributeWithName:@"postdate"
                    stringValue:[df stringFromDate:now]];
    DDXMLElement *posttime =
        [DDXMLElement attributeWithName:@"posttime"
                    stringValue:[tf stringFromDate:now]];
    NSArray *attributes =
        [NSArray arrayWithObjects:postdate, posttime, nil];
    DDXMLElement *subjectNode =
        [DDXMLElement elementWithName:@"subject"
                        stringValue:subject];
    DDXMLElement *bodyNode =
        [DDXMLElement elementWithName:@"body"
                        stringValue:body];
    NSArray *children =
        [NSArray arrayWithObjects:subjectNode, bodyNode, nil];
    DDXMLElement *doc =
        [DDXMLElement elementWithName:@"newsitem"
                            children:children
                            attributes:attributes];
    NSString *xml = [doc XMLString];
    return xml;
}
```

This version, if passed the same data as we used before, produces identical XML. So why go to the trouble of building up all those DOM structures when a simple format will do? Well, one reason is that using DOM makes sure that you don't leave out a quotation mark or angle bracket, or forget an end tag, producing bad XML.

But there's a much more important reason, which is the same reason you never use format strings to create SQL statements, it's too easy to inject garbage into the payload. Let's compare the two methods again, but with slightly more complex data (newlines and indents have been added to improve readability):

```
By Format:
<newsitem postdate="2011-07-26" posttime="11:23">
    <subject>This is a test subject<subject>
    <body>
        Buggy whips are cool & neat, > all the rest, aren't they?
    </body>
</newsitem>

By DOM:
<newsitem postdate="2011-07-26" posttime="11:23">
    <subject>This is a test subject</subject>
    <body>
      Buggy whips are cool &amp; neat, &gt; all the rest, aren't they?
    </body>
</newsitem>
```

Oh my, look at all the illegal XML characters in the middle of our payload, just waiting to break any innocent XML parser waiting on the other end. By contrast, the example using DOM construction has appropriately escaped any dangerous content.

The decision as to whether to use formatting or DOM construction isn't absolute. If you have good control of the data you're sending, and can be absolutely sure that no XML-invalid characters will be contained inside the parameters, formatting can be a real time- and code-saver. But it is inherently more dangerous than using a DOM, and you also have to deal with pesky problems such as escaping all your quote signs. I've used both techniques where appropriate, but I'm starting to lean more heavily toward DOM construction these days.

One last item: once you have the XML, how do you send it in a POST? The code is fairly simple; it's almost identical to the NSURLConnection code to do a GET. An example can be seen in Example 4-9.

Example 4-9. Posting data using NSURLConnection

```
-(void) sendNewsToServer:(NSString *) payload {
    NSURL *url = [NSURL URLWithString:@"http://thisis.a.bogus/url"];
    NSMutableURLRequest *request = [NSMutableURLRequest
                                    requestWithURL:url];
    [request setHTTPMethod:@"POST"];
    NSMutableDictionary *headers =
      [NSMutableDictionary dictionaryWithDictionary:[request allHTTPHeaderFields]];
    [headers setValue:@"text/xml" forKey:@"Content-Type"];
```

```
[request setAllHTTPHeaderFields:headers];
[request setTimeoutInterval:30];
NSData *body = [payload dataUsingEncoding:NSUTF8StringEncoding];
[request setHTTPBody:[NSMutableData dataWithData:body]];
[NSURLConnection sendAsynchronousRequest:request
                               queue:[NSOperationQueue currentQueue]
               completionHandler:^(NSURLResponse *response,
                                    NSData *data, NSError *error) {
                   if (error != nil) {
                       [self handleError:error.description];
                   } else {
                       [self displayResponse:data];
                   }
               }];
}
```

The only additional bits we need to do are to call `setHTTPBody`, add a content type using `setAllHTTPHeaderFields`, and use `setHTTPMethod` to indicate this is a POST. In all other ways, this acts just like a normal request, including the block handler and how response data is handled.

Once More, with JSON

Now that you know the basics of how to get XML back and forth to servers, it's time to move on something a little more 21st century. One side effect of the rise of HTML5, AJAX, CSS, and all the other cool web technologies is that there are now a bunch of client-friendly JSON-speaking services out there that your application can leverage.

JSON is definitely the new kid on the block in the enterprise, and large companies are just starting to embrace it (my company has been using it in some of our newer products for about a year now). The big advantages that JSON brings are a lightweight syntax and easy integration into JavaScript. But how about iOS?

Again, until recently, I would have recommended a third-party library. There's a perfectly serviceable third party library out there, called SBJSON. You can find it at *https://github.com/stig/json-framework/* and once again, the site provides detailed instructions on how to install the package into your application. You'll still need it if iOS 4 compatibility is an issue to you, but if you can make iOS 5 your minimum version, you can use the JSON support that's now integrated into iOS.

We already have an HTTP connection framework in place, in the form of the `NSURL Connection` class, so all we're really doing is changing how we generate and parse our payloads. Once again, our web service team is off taking long lunches, so we'll have to test against a public service, in this case the GeoNames geographical names database. The GeoNames API takes all of its parameters on the URL, and returns a JSON payload as the response. So for the request *http://api.geonames.org/postalCodeLookupJSON ?postalcode=03038&country=AT&username=buggywhipco*, you'll get back a payload that looks like:

```
{"postalcodes":
  [
    {
      "adminName2":"Rockingham",
      "adminCode2":"015",
      "postalcode":"03038",
      "adminCode1":"NH",
      "countryCode":"US",
      "lng":-71.301971,
      "placeName":"Derry",
      "lat":42.887404,
      "adminName1":"New Hampshire"
    }
  ]
}
```

Basically, it's an array of postal code records, with a name of fields inside it. To see how we can access this data in iOS, we'll add another button to the tab bar, and add the code shown in Example 4-10 to the controller.

Example 4-10. Making a request that returns JSON

```objc
- (IBAction)lookupZipCode:(id)sender {
    NSURL *url = [WebServiceEndpointGenerator getZipCodeEndpointForZipCode:@"03038"
                                              country:@"US"
                                              username:@"buggywhipco"];
    NSURLRequest *request = [NSURLRequest requestWithURL:url];
    [NSURLConnection sendAsynchronousRequest:request
                               queue:[NSOperationQueue currentQueue]
                   completionHandler:^(NSURLResponse *response,
                                       NSData *data, NSError *error) {
                       if (error != nil) {
                           [self handleError:error.description];
                       } else {
                           [self gotZipCode:data];
                       }
                   }];
}

- (void)gotZipCode:(NSData *)data
{
    NSError *error;
    NSDictionary *json =
      [NSJSONSerialization JSONObjectWithData:data options:0 error:&error];
    if (error != nil) {
        [self handleError:error.description];
        return;
    }
        NSArray *postalCodes = [json valueForKey:@"postalcodes"];
        if ([postalCodes count] == 0) {
            NSLog(@"No postal codes found for requested code");
            return;
        }
        for (NSDictionary *postalCode in postalCodes) {
            NSLog(@"Postal Code: %@", [postalCode valueForKey:@"postalcode"]);
```

```
NSLog(@"City: %@", [postalCode valueForKey:@"placeName"]);
NSLog(@"County: %@", [postalCode valueForKey:@"adminName2"]);
NSLog(@"State: %@", [postalCode valueForKey:@"adminName1"]);
NSString *latitudeString =
    [postalCode valueForKey:@"lat"];
NSString *northSouth = @"N";
if ([latitudeString characterAtIndex:0]== '-') {
    northSouth = @"S";
    latitudeString =
        [latitudeString substringFromIndex:1];
    }
float latitude = [latitudeString floatValue];
NSLog(@"Latitude: %4.2f%@",latitude, northSouth);
NSString *longitudeString =
    [postalCode valueForKey:@"lng"];
NSString *eastWest = @"E";
if ([longitudeString characterAtIndex:0]== '-') {
    eastWest = @"W";
    longitudeString =
        [longitudeString substringFromIndex:1];
    }
float longitude = [longitudeString floatValue];
NSLog(@"Longitude: %4.2f%@", longitude, eastWest);
    }
}
```

So, what have we got going on here? The request side is pretty straightforward: we generate a URL endpoint (the generator does pretty much what you'd expect it to do), and submit the request. When we get a response back, we check for error, and then use a method in the NSJSONSerialization class called JSONObjectWithData to parse the JSON.

The iOS 5 JSON implementation uses dictionaries, arrays, and strings to store the parsed JSON values. We look for the postalcodes value in the top level dictionary, which should contain an NSArray of postal codes. If we find it, we iterate over the array, and pluck out the individual values, printing them to the log. There's even a little extra code to turn the latitude and longitude into more human-readable versions with E/W and N/S values.

There's only one problem with the code as currently written: it will throw an exception when you run it. If you look closely at the original JSON, you'll see that's because the lat and lng values don't have double quotes around them. As a result, the objects that will be put into the dictionary for them will be NSDecimalNumber objects, not NSString. Thus, all the string manipulation code will fail. We can fix the problem easily enough:

```
NSDecimalNumber *latitudeNum =
    [postalCode valueForKey:@"lat"];
float latitude = [latitudeNum floatValue];
NSString *northSouth = @"N";
if (latitude < 0) {
    northSouth = @"S";
    latitude = - latitude;
```

```
    }
    NSLog(@"Latitude: %4.2f%@",
        latitude, northSouth);
    NSDecimalNumber *longitudeNum =
        [postalCode valueForKey:@"lng"];
    float longitude = [longitudeNum floatValue];
    NSString *eastWest = @"E";
    if (longitude < 0) {
        eastWest = @"W";
        longitude = - longitude;
    }
    NSLog(@"Longitude: %4.2f%@",
        longitude, eastWest);
```

The reason that I made that deliberate mistake is to emphasize a point about JSON serialization, which is that you have to look closely at the shape of the JSON that gets returned, and know what to expect at any particular point in the tree. Running the corrected code generates good data in the log:

```
BuggyWhipChat[9811:b603] Postal Code: 03038
BuggyWhipChat[9811:b603] City: Derry
BuggyWhipChat[9811:b603] County: Rockingham
BuggyWhipChat[9811:b603] State: New Hampshire
BuggyWhipChat[9811:b603] Latitude: 42.89N
BuggyWhipChat[9811:b603] Longitude: 71.30W
```

Having to generate JSON is somewhat less frequent a task, but it's equally simple to do. Simply use `NSDictionary`, `NSArray`, `NSString`, `NSDecimalNumber` and so on to construct the payload that you wish to send, then use the corollary method `dataWithJSONObject` of the `NSJSONSerialization` class, which will return the JSON `NSData` that corresponds to the structure.

SOAP on a Rope

So far, we've been dealing with modern, fairly light-weight web service protocols. Alas, in many enterprise companies, SOAP is still the name of the game. SOAP has a big advantage in that you can take a WSDL file and (theoretically) generate client bindings in a variety of languages and operating systems, and they will all be able to successfully communicate with the server.

The reality is somewhat less rosy. Things are certainly better than they were a few years ago, when getting a Java client to talk to an ASP.NET SOAP server could drive you insane. These days, the impedance mismatches of data types and incomplete data bindings are largely a thing of the past. What hasn't changed is the God-awful bindings that you can end up with, especially if you annotate classes and let the framework generate the WSDL, as is the habit in many projects. And who can blame them, since WSDLs are one of the most unpleasant file specifications to author?

The reality of life, however, is that there's a good chance you may need to consume a SOAP server as part of an iOS application. Luckily, there's good tooling available to help. Just as there is wsdl2java to create Java bindings for SOAP, there's a tool called WSDL2ObjC that will create all the classes to bind iOS applications. You can download it from *http://code.google.com/p/wsdl2objc/*, and unlike the other tools we've discussed in this section, it's not a library but a Mac utility. When you download the tool and run it, you are presented with a window with two text fields and a button (Figure 4-4). You put a URI specification for a WSDL file in the first text field, the second specifies the directory that you want your generated code to be placed into. When you click the button, you get a directory full of files that you can add to your iOS project, and use to call the web service.

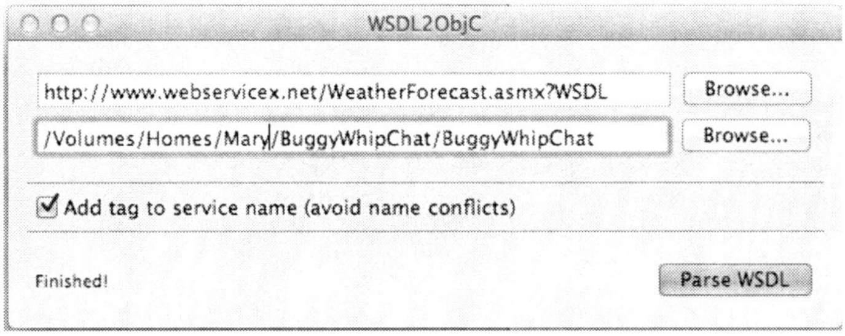

Figure 4-4. Generating a SOAP binding using WSDL2ObjC

In this example, we're consuming another weather service, because we really care about the weather here at BuggyWhipCo. An extra-humid day can ruin an entire batch of lacquered buggy whips, you know! In any event, we have the WSDL URI for a SOAP-based weather service, and we've used it to generate a whole bunch of files that support the binding to the service. If you look in the directory you generated your files into, you'll see something like this:

```
NSDate+ISO8601Parsing.h
NSDate+ISO8601Parsing.m
NSDate+ISO8601Unparsing.h
NSDate+ISO8601Unparsing.m
USAdditions.h
USAdditions.m
USGlobals.h
USGlobals.m
WeatherSvc.h
WeatherSvc.m
xsd.h
xsd.m
```

With the exception of the two *WeatherSvc* files, everything else is standard and common to all SOAP web services you generate, and if you have more than one service you bind to, you'll only need one copy of those files (if you generate all your services into the same directory, this should happen automatically).

Well, that was certainly easy! Except, actually, we're just getting started. As anyone who has ever used SOAP bindings knows, making them work involves a bunch of guesswork and a menagerie of intermediate objects of no particularly obvious purpose. Let's look at the code that you'd need to write in order to consume this service, shown in Example 4-11.

Example 4-11. Consuming a SOAP web service

```
- (IBAction)showSOAPWeather:(id)sender {
    WeatherSoapBinding *binding =
        [WeatherSvc WeatherSoapBinding];
    binding.logXMLInOut = YES;
    WeatherSvc_GetWeather *params = [[WeatherSvc_GetWeather alloc] init];
    params.City = @"Derry, NH";
    WeatherSoapBindingResponse  *response =
    [binding
     GetWeatherUsingParameters:params];
    for (id bodyPart in response.bodyParts) {
        if ([bodyPart isKindOfClass:[SOAPFault class]]) {
            NSLog(@"Got error: %@",
                ((SOAPFault *)bodyPart).simpleFaultString);
            continue;
        }

        if ([bodyPart isKindOfClass:
            [WeatherSvc_GetWeatherResponse class]]) {
            WeatherSvc_GetWeatherResponse *response = bodyPart;
            NSLog(@"Forecast: %@", response.GetWeatherResult);
        }
    }
}
```

The general pattern here, as with most SOAP bindings, is that you get a binding object (which has all the information about things such as the URI of the service). Then you get a request object, set all the parameters of the request, then call the appropriate method on the binding (in this case, `GetWeatherUsingParameters`), handing in the request. There are two versions of each request method, one synchronous (the one we're using in this example), and one asynchronous (which uses the same kind of callback mechanism we've used in the JSON and XML examples). We also set the `logXMLInOut` flag to true, so we'll get a look at what we're sending and receiving in pure SOAP form, this can be very helpful figuring out where data is hiding in the response.

When the response returns, you have to iterate over the body parts, checking for SOAP faults. If the body part isn't a SOAP fault, you have to cast it to the appropriate object. And here's where the fun begins, because there's nothing to tell you what the possible types are, except for diving through the generated code looking for where the elements are populated. But, if you do it all right, you'll get results.

```
2011-11-18 08:16:17.365 BuggyWhipChat[69775:fb03] Forecast: Sunny
```

Looks like nice beach weather! If you're getting the feeling that I'm not a big fan of SOAP, you wouldn't be wrong. And, mind you, what we just saw is an extremely simple SOAP call, with no authentication and very simple request and response objects. I have not tried to make WSDL2ObjC work with WS-Security, although there is anecdotal evidence that it is possible. In any event, the good news is that SOAP on iOS isn't impossible.

A Final Caution

Whenever you are relying on third-party libraries, you're at the mercy of the maintainers. If it is a proprietary library, you have to hope that they will keep the tool up to date, and that it will not be broken by the next update to XCode or iOS.

For open source libraries, things are a little better. If the committers on the project aren't willing or able to update the project, you have the source and can take a swing at it yourself. Depending on the license, this may mean that you have to make the sources to your changes available for download.

This is not some abstract warning, I know for a fact that most of the tools mentioned in the chapter do not work in projects that are using the Automatic Reference Count compiler feature in iOS 5. This means that you're going to be faced with the choice of trying to get the libraries working with ARC, or building them as non-ARC static libraries that are called from your ARC project. One factor to consider when choosing libraries is how active the developer community is, and how often new versions come out. WSDL2ObjC, for example, seems relatively moribund, and might slip into orphan status in the future.

With our application cheerfully (if uselessly) talking to web services, we should think about how we're going to test it. That's what you'll learn in Chapter 5.

Testing Enterprise iOS Applications

If there's one philosophy that has become entrenched in the DNA of software development in recent memory, it's that testing is crucial. For some organizations, it means comprehensive unit testing, for others a full-on TDD approach with continuous integration and regression testing. But the chances are that you're not going to be shipping your iOS application out the door without some significant test infrastructure.

Beyond simple unit testing, you also should have testing of the running application, which offers its own challenges. Not only do you need to have a testing framework that can successfully exercise your UI, but you also have to make sure that all your other integration components (such as backend servers and databases) are in a consistent state every time you run the tests.

Recently, more advanced metrics such as cyclic complexity numbers (CCN) have become en vogue. They recognize that just because code is fully tested doesn't mean that it's well written. On the other hand, developers can end up gaming the system to get lower CCN numbers, at the cost of code quality. We'll take a look at how to generate CCN metrics automatically, later in the chapter.

It's worth noting here that the various testing frameworks have, in my opinion, been the most poorly maintained and casually broken parts of the SDK over the time that I've been developing. Apple changes how (and if!) test frameworks operate without notice, and sometimes apparently at random. Developers with automated test frameworks pray to their chosen deity before taking an XCode update, because you never know what may and may not work afterwards. With that in mind, be aware that anything you see here is subject to change, and just because you set something up one way today doesn't mean that it will work the same way tomorrow. The general principles outlined here should hold true, however.

Unit Testing iOS Applications

Creating unit tests is probably the most straightforward part of iOS testing, because OCUnit has been a part of XCode for a long time (so it's pretty well documented). With recent releases of XCode, things have been improved further, such as by running the tests on the simulator rather than at compile time, which makes them easier to debug, and offers up a powerful new alternative to the creaky `UIAutomationTesting` framework, something I'll get to shortly.

Certain things had been broken, however—most notably the generation of code coverage statistics using the gcov library. When iOS 4 went to using LLVM as the default compiler, gcov was broken, but it has returned from the dead in iOS 5. I'll talk a bit about gcov and CoverStory later in this section.

Setting Up an OCUnit Target

In any event, you get asked if you want to create a unit test target when you first create a project. If you don't, you can add one later by doing a simple "Add Target" and picking "Cocoa Touch Unit Testing Bundle" (Figure 5-1).

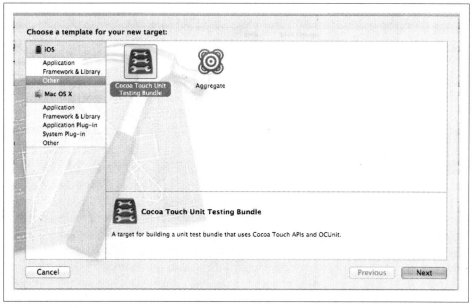

Figure 5-1. Adding an OCUnit target to your project

Once you have a testing target, you can immediately try running it, since the default template creates a single unit test file with a single failing test case. You'll eventually want to have multiple files of tests; you can create more by dropping new "Objective-C test case class" files into the unit test target.

There are a few things to point out immediately. Firstly, you need to make sure that the testing target has access to all the classes, frameworks, and resources that the test cases will need to run. You can set them up in the Build Phases tab of the target info (Figure 5-2).

Figure 5-2. Adding dependencies to a test target

This used to be a lot more of a pain in the butt than it is now. Until recently, OCUnit tests ran at compile time, and therefore couldn't make use of things in the framework libraries, or any class in your code that included them. You had to carefully manage which files went into which target, or your unit test target wouldn't compile.

Well, all that has changed. You can now make your whole honking application a dependency of your unit test target, and have access to anything in it, as we'll see later. But for the moment, just know that if your test target sets a target dependency on your application, you should be all set.

Once you have the test target all set up, it's time to write some unit tests. Remember, unit tests are intended to test the functionality in a single class, and purists insist on using techniques like dependency injection and mock classes to isolate logic down to a single class. This has the advantage of letting you test your code in a clean-room, as it were, but requires you to create a lot more test framework. It's not my place to prescribe a unit testing approach, but I'll say that I find that making some compromises here can let you test effectively without having to recreate the entire outside world in mocks.

We have a few classes it would be useful to unit test from the Buggy Whip Chat application (you first saw these back in Chapter 4), namely the URL endpoint generators. So, to begin our testing effort, let's tackle them.

We start, as described above, by adding a new unit test class to our unit test target. Since we're testing the `WebServiceEndpointGenerator` class, we'll call it `TestWeb ServiceEndpointGenerator`. For some reason (as of this writing, as with everything in the book), creating a unit test project gives you a nice clean sample test case file, but adding a new test class gives you the old template, full of conditionals for in-app vs. static testing that don't really apply anymore since unit tests now always run on the simulator, not at compile time. So, the first thing we can do is to strip out all the conditionalization logic in the header and code files, leaving them ending much more like the sample file you get with the target. When we're done, they should look like the code in Example 5-1.

Example 5-1. The header and code files for a bare test case

```
////  TestWebServiceEndpointGenerator.h

#import <SenTestingKit/SenTestingKit.h>
#import <UIKit/UIKit.h>

@interface TestWebServiceEndpointGenerator : SenTestCase

@end


////  TestWebServiceEndpointGenerator.m

#import "TestWebServiceEndpointGenerator.h"

@implementation TestWebServiceEndpointGenerator

@end
```

The first method to test is the `getForecastWebServiceEndpoint` method. So that we can do negative as well as positive testing, the method has been rewritten slightly to add some argument checking at the top:

```
+(NSURL *) getForecastWebServiceEndpoint:
       (NSString *) zipcode
       startDate:(NSDate *) startDate
       endDate:(NSDate *) endDate {
    if ((zipcode == NULL) || (startDate == NULL) ||
      (endDate == NULL)) {
```

```
            NSException *exception =
                [NSException
                   exceptionWithName:
                     @"Missing Argument Exception"
                   reason:@"An argument was missing"
                   userInfo:nil];
            @throw exception;
        }
        if ([endDate compare:startDate] == NSOrderedAscending) {
            NSException *exception =
              [NSException exceptionWithName:@"Date Order Exception"
                 reason:@"The start date can not be after the end date"
                 userInfo:nil];
            @throw exception;
        }
```

Now we have some nice juicy argument checking we can use for negative tests. But since we're optimistic by nature, let's write the positive test first, shown in Example 5-2.

Example 5-2. Writing positive test cases

```
NSDate *testStartDate;
NSDate *testEndDate;

-(void) setUp {
    NSDateFormatter *df = [NSDateFormatter new];
    [df setDateFormat:@"YY-MM-dd"];
    testStartDate = [df dateFromString:@"2011-08-01"];
    testEndDate = [df dateFromString:@"2011-08-02"];
}

-(void) testGetForecastWebServiceEndpointSuccess {
    NSURL *url =
        [WebServiceEndpointGenerator
                    getForecastWebServiceEndpoint:@"03038"
                    startDate:testStartDate
                    endDate:testEndDate];
    STAssertNotNil(url, @"No URL returned");
    NSString *correctURL = @"";
    NSString *urlString = [url absoluteString];
    STAssertEqualObjects(@"", urlString,
      @"The generated URL, %@, did not match the \
        expected URL,
      %@", urlString, correctURL);}
```

Breaking this down, we start by defining two variables to hold a start and end date, since we'll be using them in a lot of the test cases, and we don't want to have to create them fresh in each one. Every test case class has a setUp and tearDown method that you can override, which will be run before the test cases start and after they end, respectively. It's a good place to make sure all your state is reset, and to initialize common data that will be needed by the class. We can place our code to create good test dates there.

The actual test case itself just calls the method under test with good data, and then makes sure that we got a good value back, and that the URL string matches what we expect. All of the unit test assertions are documented, but they generally follow the pattern of a test condition, an error message that will be used with the `NSString` `stringWithFormat` message, and the arguments to the formatter. In this case, we use `STAssertNotNil` and `STAssertEqualObjects`. You should understand that `STAssertEqualObjects` and `STAssertEquals` have different behaviors: the former uses the `equals` message, while the latter tests for literally object equality.

If you run this test as is (by selecting Product→Test, typing ⌘-U, or holding the run icon and selecting Test), it will fail, as shown in Figure 5-3.

Figure 5-3. A failing test run

This is because we're testing the generated URL string against the empty string. So where do we get a good string to test it against? In pure TDD, we would have figured out what string we should expect before we wrote the code and the test would have tested for it. In lazy man's TDD, we can run the test against a known bad string, copy the good string out of the error log by right-clicking on the error in the navigator and selecting "copy", inspect it and make sure that it looks correct, then paste it into the "expected" string part of the test.

Happy path testing is all well and good, but as you probably know, the world is full of sad, broken paths. To round out the tests, we can write a number of negative cases, shown in Example 5-3.

Example 5-3. Writing negative test cases

```
-(void) testGetForecastWebServiceEndpointMissingZip {
    @try {
        [WebServiceEndpointGenerator
          getForecastWebServiceEndpoint:nil
          startDate:testStartDate endDate:testEndDate];
    } @catch (NSException * e) {
        STAssertEqualObjects(@"Missing Argument Exception",
            e.name, @"Wrong exception type");
```

```
        return;
    }
    STFail(@"Call did not generate exception");
}

-(void) testGetForecastWebServiceEndpointMissingStartDate {
    @try {
        [WebServiceEndpointGenerator
            getForecastWebServiceEndpoint:@"03038"
            startDate:nil endDate:testEndDate];
    } @catch (NSException * e) {
        STAssertEqualObjects(@"Missing Argument Exception",
            e.name, @"Wrong exception type");
        return;
    }
    STFail(@"Call did not generate exception");
}

-(void) testGetForecastWebServiceEndpointMissingEndDate {
    @try {
        [WebServiceEndpointGenerator
            getForecastWebServiceEndpoint:@"03038"
            startDate:testStartDate endDate:nil];
    } @catch (NSException * e) {
        STAssertEqualObjects(@"Missing Argument Exception",
            e.name, @"Wrong exception type");
        return;
    }
    STFail(@"Call did not generate exception");
}

-(void) testGetForecastWebServiceEndpointDatesInWrongOrder {
    @try {
        [WebServiceEndpointGenerator
            getForecastWebServiceEndpoint:@"03038"
            startDate:testEndDate endDate:testStartDate];
    } @catch (NSException * e) {
        STAssertEqualObjects(@"Date Order Exception",
            e.name, @"Wrong exception type");
        return;
    }
    STFail(@"Call did not generate exception");
}
```

The interesting bit in these test cases is that, because what we're interested in is whether or not the tested method throws an exception, what we do is wrap the invocation of the method in a try block, and if the exception is thrown, compare the exception name with the name we were expecting to see. If the name is wrong, the assert will fail. If the exception is not thrown, we won't return out of the test in the catch clause, and will explicitly fail.

Generating Code Coverage Metrics

These days, it's not enough to write good unit tests: you also need to prove that you're covering all the code with them. As previously mentioned, you can use the gcov library to produce code coverage results from your unit tests. To do this, turn on the Generate Test Coverage Files flag in the Build Settings of your unit test target, as shown in Figure 5-4.

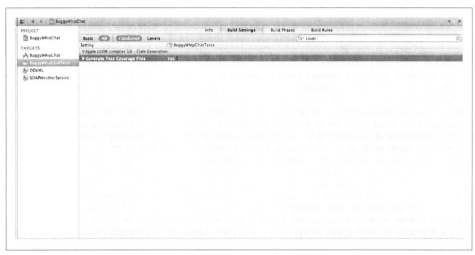

Figure 5-4. Turning on code coverage in XCode

Once you've turned on code coverage support and run your unit tests, you're going to end up with a bunch of files with gcda and gcno extensions somewhere. Perhaps in your project directory; more likely in some place like *~/Library/Developer/Xcode/DerivedData*. Unfortunately, these files are next to useless to try and interpret visually. Fortunately, there are good tools such as CoverStory to do all the hard work for you.

CoverStory is available at *http://code.google.com/p/coverstory/*, and is a normal Mac OS X application. When you run it, you can use the File→Open command to point it at a directory (or tree of directories) containing your code coverage files. It then opens up and displays a listing of your code, with unrun code shown in red, and counts next to each line showing how many times each line ran (Figure 5-5).

CoverStory also gives you a list of files on the left-hand side, along with code coverage percentages, so you can see how your code is doing, coverage-wise, and find under-covered files.

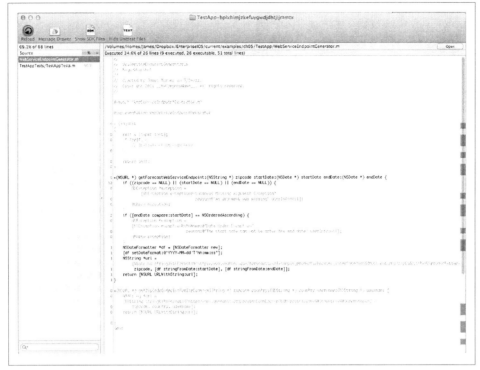

Figure 5-5. An example of a CoverStory session

Generating Code Complexity Metrics

Over the last few years, code complexity metrics have become the hot new measure of code goodness. Simply put, cyclomatic complexity numbers (CCN) are a measure of how many ways there are of getting through a given piece of code. The more conditional code you have in a method, the deeper you nest your if statements, the more looping you're doing, the higher your numbers are going to be.

Different organizations have different acceptable levels of complexity. For example, a company might mandate that any new code must have a CCN lower than 20, while old code must be refactored if the number is higher than 50. Getting numbers down typically involves breaking up large methods into smaller ones, and is generally a good thing, although I've seen cases where code actually ended up less readable as a result of trying to knock down high CCN numbers.

In the Java world, tools like Coverity are routinely used to generate CCN metrics, and even to fail builds based on them. In my searches, I've only found one good tool to compute CCN metrics for Objective-C, and it's just a Python script that a guy named Terry Yinzhe threw together under the Apache license. It's called *hfcca13.py*, and it's included in the example code for the book (see "How to Contact Us" on page ix).

Using it is very simple. Simply invoke it with a list of the source (not header) files that you wish to have analyzed, and it will spit out the result to the command line. For example, running it against our source tree gives results like this:

```
$ ./hfcca13.py `find ChatAPI -name "*.m" -print`
================================================================
NLOC    CCN    token           function@line@file
----------------------------------------------------------------
    9     2      10 init@13@ChatAPI/ChatAPI/GoogleTalkAPI.m
    6     1       4 setUp@13@ChatAPI/ChatAPITests/ChatAPITests.m
    6     1       4 tearDown@20@ChatAPI/ChatAPITests/ChatAPITests.m
    4     1       3 testExample@27@ChatAPI/ChatAPITests/ChatAPITests.m
----------------------------------------------------------------
2 file analyzed.
================================================================
LOC     Avg.NLOC AvgCCN Avg.ttoken  function_cnt    file
----------------------------------------------------------------
   24     9      2       10          1         ChatAPI/ChatAPI/GoogleTalkAPI.m
   33     5      1        3          3         ChatAPI/ChatAPITests/ChatAPITests.m

!!!! Warnings (CCN > 15) !!!!
================================================================
NLOC    CCN    token           function@file
----------------------------------------------------------------
Total warning: (0/4, 0.0%)
```

As you can see, we're being good little programmers, and have no methods with CCN values above 15. The script takes a number of parameters to tweak the behavior, including setting the warning threshold for the CCN value. At work, we've integrated the script into our Hudson build, and the build automatically breaks if it finds values above a certain level.

Creating UI Tests (The Old and Painful Way)

If you want to test your UI, the traditional way (at least for the last year or so) has been to use the UIAutomation Framework. The UIAutomation Framework works in conjunction with the Instruments tool. You create JavaScript files that can be used to access and poke at the UI elements of the application, within some fairly restrictive bounds, and with some nasty bugs to watch out for. I was never so happy a developer as the day I was able to hand off test script creation to our QA team, because it was excruciating work to create them.

To begin, we need to do some setup work in our project. The framework uses the Accessibility label property of UI elements to refer to them in the JavaScript, so the first step is to mark up the elements in Interface Builder (shown in Figure 5-6). However, there's a bug that will cause everything to go pear-shaped very quickly if you ever assign an accessibility label to a view of any kind, so you may be better off without it.

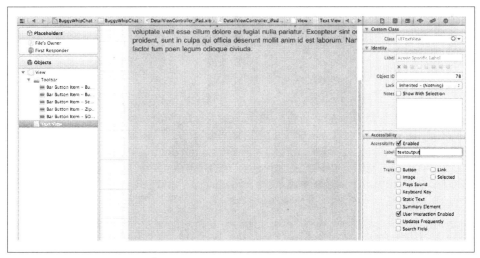

Figure 5-6. Labeling elements for scripting

Alas, many of the elements on the screen don't have accessibility labels, so you have to access them through more arcane methods. As a example, let's look at a test that looks for the zip code button in the toolbar, presses it, and then sees if it gets a good value back (Example 5-4).

Example 5-4. A sample UIAutomation script

```
UIALogger.logStart("Find Toolbar");
var target = UIATarget.localTarget();
var window = target.frontMostApp().mainWindow();
window.logElementTree();
var toolbars = window.toolbars();
if (toolbars.length != 1) {
    UILogger.logFail("Did not find toolbar");
}

UIALogger.logStart("Find Output View");
var outputViews = window.textViews();
if (outputViews.length == 0) {
    UIALogger.logFail("Did not find output textview");
}
var outputView = outputViews[0];

UIALogger.logStart("Find Button");
var buttons = toolbars[0].buttons();
var zipButton = buttons["Zip Code"];
if (zipButton == null) {
    UILogger.logFail("Did not find zipcode button");
}

UIALogger.logStart("Test Zipcode Button");
zipButton.tap();
```

```
var result =
    outputView.withValueForKey(
        "Postal Code: 03038\nCity: ... Longitude: 71.30W\n",
        "value");
if (result == null) {
    UILogger.logFail("Did not get expected result");
}
```

So what have we got going on here? The `UIALogger.logStart` call signals to the framework that we're about to start a test. The next two lines are boilerplate, and gain access to the currently visible window of the application. The `logElementTree` call is useful to put in during test development: it dumps a tree view of all the UI elements below the specified one (in this case, the window) to the log, so that you can figure out how to navigate to specific elements in your test code.

Next, we get a list of all the toolbars on the window (there should only be one, something we test for and fail if untrue). We also look for the TextView that we use for output, and the button inside the toolbar called "Zip Code". Here we see one of the weaknesses of the framework—you need to access the buttons by their label text, which means that these tests will fail if the test is run in a different language. You can also try to get the button positionally, but this means that if you add a button, the test may break.

Once the test has access to the button, we have the test tap it, and check to see if the string placed in the results view is correct. But we can't just tap the button and then use the `value()` method on the output view to check it, because the web service will almost certainly not have returned yet, so the text in the view will be the old text. Instead, we need to use the `withValueForKey` method, specifying "value" as the key. The way that this method works is that it searches for an element which satisfies the criteria, waiting until a specified timeout (which you can configure) has elapsed before failing (and returning null). So, if the output view value becomes equal to the test string before the timeout occurs, the view will be returned and the test against null will fail.

This kind of programmatic acrobatics is typical of what you have to go through when using the UIAutomation Framework. It is extremely poorly documented by Apple, tends to be very fragile and occasionally non-intuitive, and is (unfortunately) the only officially supported game in town.

Anyway, once you have your test script, you fire up Instruments, and select the Automation template (Figure 5-7). Once at the main screen, use the target pulldown at the top to select the simulator version of your application build (which may be hiding down inside of your *~/Library/Developer/DerviedData* hierarchy), select the script on the script pane, and hit the record button (Figure 5-8).

When you run the test, the Script Log will show you the results. One thing that you'll quickly notice is that the test never stops; you have to hit the record button again to stop it. For this reason (among others), you can't use these tests from the command line as part of an automated build process.

Figure 5-7. Starting Instruments

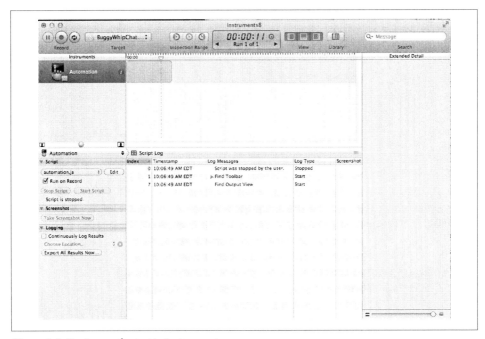

Figure 5-8. Setting up the test in Instruments

One thing you can do is to throw other instruments such as memory leak detectors on in parallel with your automation test, which will allow you to profile your application over time to make sure you don't introduce issues down the road.

Because of the awkwardness, fragility, and slowness of the framework, it would be nice if there were alternatives, and there are. They just aren't officially supported.

UI Testing Using OCUnit

In theory, now that OCUnit tests run in the simulator, you could write your UI tests using OCUnit and be done with the UIAutomation framework. The only problem is that until recently, if you tried to do this, you'd get a message saying that testing UI with OCUnit was only supported on physical devices. In other words, if you wanted to do this, you'd need to run it with a tethered phone or pad attached, which is pretty non-optimal.

Recently, things have changed. Now, if you create a Cocoa Touch Unit Testing Target, and then go into the build settings for the target and set the Test Host parameter to `$(BUNDLE_LOADER)`, you can run tests that directly manipulate the UI. You can see how this is set in Figure 5-9.

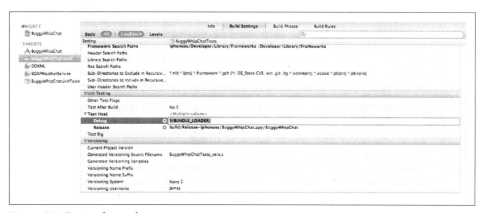

Figure 5-9. Setting the test host

With the tests set to run against the test host, we can now write UI OCUnit tests, such as the one in Example 5-5.

Example 5-5. A Cocoa Touch unit test

```
#import "BuggyWhipChatTests.h"
#import "BuggyWhipChatAppDelegate.h"
#import "RootViewController.h"
#import "DetailViewController.h"

@implementation BuggyWhipChatTests
```

```objc
BuggyWhipChatAppDelegate *delegate;

- (void)setUp{
    [super setUp];
    delegate =
        [[UIApplication sharedApplication] delegate];
}

- (void)tearDown{
    [super tearDown];
}

- (void) testUIElementsPresent {
    RootViewController *controller =
        delegate.rootViewController;
    STAssertNotNil(controller,
            @"Root view controller not found");
    if ([[UIDevice currentDevice] userInterfaceIdiom] ==
            UIUserInterfaceIdiomPad) {
        STAssertNotNil(controller.detailViewController,
            @"Detail view controller not found on iPad");
    }
}

-(void) testSOAPWeather {
    RootViewController *controller =
            delegate.rootViewController;
    DetailViewController *detail =
            controller.detailViewController;
    detail.outputView.text = @"";
    [detail showSOAPWeather:nil];
    int i;
    for (i = 0; i < 30; i++) {
        [[NSRunLoop currentRunLoop] runUntilDate:
                [NSDate dateWithTimeIntervalSinceNow: 1]];
        if ([detail.outputView.text length] > 0) {
            break;
        }
    }
    STAssertTrue([detail.outputView.text length] > 0,
                @"Detail view is blank");
}

-(void) testZipCode {
    RootViewController *controller =
        delegate.rootViewController;
    DetailViewController *detail =
        controller.detailViewController;
    detail.outputView.text = @"";
    [detail lookupZipCode:nil];
    int i;
    for (i = 0; i < 30; i++) {
        [[NSRunLoop currentRunLoop] runUntilDate:
                [NSDate dateWithTimeIntervalSinceNow: 1]];
```

```
        if ([detail.outputView.text length] > 0) {
            break;
        }
    }
    STAssertTrue([detail.outputView.text length] > 0,
            @"Detail view is blank");
}

@end
```

As opposed to the arcane UIAutomation framework, this is pretty straightforward. In the setup for each test, we grab a handle on the application delegate. Then in the first test, we check to make sure that we can find the root view controller—and if we're running in iPad mode, that we can find the detail controller.

In the two meaningful tests, we set the text of the output view to empty, then trigger the event handler for the button (which simulates the action of pressing the button itself). In order to let the asynchronous network request run, we go into a loop, giving the current run loop a second to execute, then checking to see if the output view has been set. If we see it is set, we break out of the loop. After the loop ends (one way or another), we test to see if we got a result.

This style of testing is much easier to create, and can be incorporated directly into the development process, rather than requiring the developer to break out into JavaScript to create the UI tests. It will also allow code coverage of UI testing.

The one current problem with UI OCUnit testing is that no one has figured out how to run it from the command line, so it can't be used as part of an automated build process. Because it uses the simulator, this will be a fragile thing even if it is enabled, because the simulator can get into funny states or hang. But even in its present state, if it continues to work, it represents a big step forward for the testing process.

Now that our app is all tested and happy, we're ready to put it up for sale. But if this is the first time you've thought about the iTunes store, you're in for a rude surprise. You need to be thinking about it from the first day of your project, which is just what the next chapter is about.

CHAPTER 6

Enterprises and the iTunes App Store

I've spent quite a bit of time talking about technical details of iOS development in the enterprise, but now I need to return to reality for a bit, and talk about some of the logistical headaches involved in large corporations that want to interact with Apple. In specific, it's time to talk go over all the cultural impedance mismatches you're likely to encounter as you shepherd your first app into the store. This chapter is structured in the form of a countdown to launch, with a list of all the things I know of that could be preparing to bite you in the butt at any given time. However, I'm sure that there are new and unique disasters that people are going to discover, so don't take this as an exhaustive list. Your mileage in (Cupertino) California may vary.

Things to Start Worrying About Immediately

So, it's day one of your new project, the first iOS project your company has ever shipped. You may not know it, but it's also going to be a chance to meet all sorts of new people inside your company that you may never have had contact with before. And that adventure starts today, because you're going to have to seek out your company's legal department.

Legal Considerations

Almost the very first thing that you're going to have to do when you sign up for a corporate iOS developer account is to accept the terms and conditions (T&Cs) of the App Store. Ask yourself, do you personally have authorization to enter into contracts on behalf of your company? I'm guessing the answer to that is no. So, before you really get started at all, you're going to need to have the T&Cs reviewed by corporate counsel, and be given approval to accept the terms on the website.

This is also a dandy time to have a conversation about what will need to happen the next time the T&Cs change, which happens with distressing regularity. Pretty much whenever any new feature is added to the store (iBooks, in-app purchases, etc.) the T&Cs change. While it may be seductively tempting to just check the "I agree" button and go on with your life, it will not amuse the lawyers in the slightest.

This is not a trivial concern. Usually, you only get a window of a few weeks to agree to new T&Cs before your account gets suspended. Imagine if you get a new set three weeks before a product launch, and your legal department decided to be slow to get approval back. These are the situations that keep the American pharmaceutical industry in business.

If you're really lucky, your legal team may come back and want to make amendments to the T&Cs before agreeing to them. I've never personally tried to get Apple to agree to a change in the stock T&Cs, so if this happens to you, let me know how it goes. I suspect with hundreds of thousands of developers to manage, your company isn't going to appear as enough of a blip on Apple's radar to get special attention.

While you're talking to the people with Esquire after their names, it's also a good time to discuss the EULA between you and your users. If you don't provide one, you get Apple's stock EULA. Almost certainly, this isn't the EULA that you will want to ship with your product. The good news is, you have until the actual go-live of your app to get your EULA in order, but it's best to get the ball rolling now. Also ask if the legal folks will want different EULAs in different countries, and if they want to have the EULA translated into different languages. You won't need to actually do this work— your translation team will—but you will need to have it available to cut and paste into the app description at the appropriate time.

If you haven't worn out your welcome by now, also find out what open source licenses are acceptable to the company, and discuss how any attribution requirements will be handled. Many applications choose to have the attributions for any open source packages they use displayed on a special tab on the Settings page for their app. There's a great little script I found, written by a Stack Overflow user called JosephH, that will automatically generate these settings pages, I've included the script and the instructions on how to use it in the downloadable files for this chapter.

Marketing Considerations

Your next stop should be to the marketing group, probably with your product manager in tow. There's not a lot of flexibility in how applications appear in the iTunes store. You can't do much formatting of the text, you get a fixed number of screen shots, and so on.

You need to communicate these limitations very clearly to your creative team, so that they can start thinking about how to best present the new app. Do they want to have an independent website that has a more glossy, polished look, with a link to the app store? Do they want to translate the app store into multiple languages (something iTunes supports)?

You should also make sure that you all agree on what the application is going to be called, and make sure that name isn't already in use. If it isn't, it's probably a good idea to get it trademarked, so that you can prevent someone's flatulence app from appearing with a similar name.

There's a bit of a delicate dance regarding reserving names in the App Store. Once you create a new app, you have 90 days to upload a binary into the store, or you lose the name forever. It's important to note that you don't need to place the app up for sale, just upload a binary. As will be discussed later in the chapter, it's a good idea to upload early and often, so this is probably not as much of an issue as it might seem, but it's important to remember that you may have a window of time where you've picked a name, but haven't reserved it yet. That's why trademarks can be your friend.

Production Considerations

Ready for your last stop? Find out who controls product ordering and fulfillment, and set up a meeting. Almost certainly, they have never encountered the kind of sales channel that iOS apps pass through, and it will require some adjustment on their part.

To begin with, you're going to have to explain to them that the concept of a Gold Master isn't going to apply to the App Store. In point of fact, there is no physical artifact that represents the version of the product you upload for sale into the App Store, because the only way to do it is from inside XCode.

This can lead to some weird circumstances. For example, you may be contractually required to ship a physical copy of the app to some customers. So what exactly is going to go on that CD? An Ad Hoc IPA file? They can't use it, since their devices won't be on the provisioning profile. A copy of the IPA that got uploaded to the App Store? You can only install those by downloading them directly from the Store. A *README.TXT* file? Believe me, you'd rather get this conversation started early, rather than be negotiating at the last moment.

Another issue to discuss is how the final production build will be created and uploaded to the store. It needs (as has been previously mentioned) to be done from XCode, which means a Mac and someone who knows how to drive it. They almost certainly do not want you uploading it from your development machine. The accommodation we came up with was to fire up XCode on the build machine (that runs Hudson), point it at the directory with the sources for the last successful build, and do an archive and upload from that.

But wait, there's more! How will the product be priced? Will it be given away, and revenue made on server licenses? Will there be volume license arrangements available? Apple has just recently added the ability to do custom volume deals with companies, so this may be something you need to discuss with your fulfillment team. What kind of sales reports will they want out of iTunes Connect? Where do the checks from Apple need to go? Make sure that you're all on the same page regarding the logistics of selling via iTunes.

Bonus Considerations

If you haven't run out of hours in the day yet, go talk to the User Experience and UI Design team that will be working with you. Make sure than have looked at Apple's UX guidelines, so they are familiar with the look and feel Apple expects in their apps.

Also, you're going to need to discuss graphic assets with them. Depending on which devices you plan to deploy on, you may need as many as four different resolutions of each image, and almost always need at least normal and 2X versions. Make sure that they know about the iOS naming conventions for the various resolutions of images, so they will name them correctly to begin with.

Things to Worry About a Month Before Launch

By now, your application should be pretty close to code freeze. That's because you're not a month before launch, you're two weeks before launch. That other two weeks is the time you should budget for the final version of the app to get reviewed by Apple, potentially rejected once for something weird, and put through the sausage grinder a second time.

Obviously, if you're not wedded to a specific shipping date, you can be a little more relaxed about things. But if you need to have the app ready to go on a specific date to, say, dovetail with press releases and a marketing campaign, it would be really good to have the app ready.

Apple will, under extraordinary circumstances, expedite reviews. We had to go to that well once, when the test server we had provisioned for Apple to test against went down right before they tried to test it, leading to a bounced review. But it's not a well you want to draw from every time you do a release, so careful planning is highly recommended.

Get a Binary into Review

If you haven't done so yet, upload a binary into iTunes Connect and start a review on it. You can have a binary reviewed without putting it up for sale, so this is a good first chance to make sure there are no problems waiting for you down the road. Of course, the app better work, not crash, etc., or it will get bounced. Frankly, if your app is still doing that stuff this close to release, it may be time to have that career-limiting conversation with your manager about slipping the ship date.

The other reason that it's a good idea to get a build approved now is that, should something go wrong with the approval of the final build, you'll have a backup (the build that was approved earlier) ready to go live in the app store that may not be perfect, but will do the job.

Double-Check App Store Readiness

Now is the time to make sure that all the legal stuff like EULAs are in place, that you have screen capture and marketing copy for the app store entry, and that any attribution notices are either in the app itself or in the App Store description.

Have a Chat With Your Support Group About Bug Reports

Depending on how you are selling the app (e.g., free with a backend license, directly sold through the App Store), you can expect to receive your bug reports from many different channels. They may show up as negative comments in the App Store. They may come in as calls to the support organization. You can get crash reports via iTunes Connect. Coordinating all this with the support organization will be complicated, and probably something they're not used to. In some companies, bug fixing is handled by a different group than mainline engineering. If so, are there qualified engineers in the organization that can diagnose and fix bugs in iOS applications?

There may also be some institutional inertia to unstick. Companies used to quarterly or half-yearly patch releases for their server products may be unaccustomed to the idea of near-instant releasability of fixes to the customers through app updates. More than once, we had conversations that started with "but what happens if they're running the last version of the software?" The idea that you could keep all your customers at the latest release (or require them to update their apps to fix problems) is very foreign to most enterprise companies.

Be aware that there's a corollary problem that instant updates can bring, which will be discussed in Chapter 8.

Things to Worry About Two Weeks Before Launch

Hopefully, you now have an approved binary in iTunes Connect, in pending status, and the code has been frozen for a couple of weeks with no significant bugs against it. Barring a catastrophic bug showing up in the next two weeks, any new bugs should be put on backlog for your 1.1 update.

Upload the Final Version to iTunes Connect

If you've been automatically inserting build numbers into your version numbers, you just need to create a new version in iTunes Connect that matches that build number, and use XCode to archive and upload the app. If you're doing it by hand, remember that the version numbers have to always increase from one version to the next, and must match between the version in the plist file and the version you create in iTunes Connect.

Once it's uploaded, it will head off for review. Make sure that if there are test servers the Apple engineers will have to use to test the app, that they are up and any necessary credentials are included in the testing notes in the version description. Believe it or not, Apple does in fact try to use your app—it's not just some automated servers somewhere scanning your code for bad API calls. I know from personal experience.

Things to Worry About One Week Before Launch

Did your application pass review? No worries, then! If not, you'll be scrambling to fix whatever caused it to bounce, pleading for an expedited review, and praying to the deity of your choice. As mentioned above, we had a bounce in the final week of our release due to a server glitch, and it was...interesting. The kind of interesting that you, many years from now, can laugh about. A quiet, hysterical kind of laugh.

When to Pull the Trigger

If you haven't discussed the actual mechanisms of "pulling the trigger" with all the concerned parties, now is a good time. Once you release an application into the store, it can take time to propagate, especially to non-US versions of the store. If it's critical to the timing of the launch that the app be available at a certain time, it may be worthwhile to "pull the trigger" the night before.

Also, now is the time to work out your launch-day plan of operations. Who is going to make sure that the app is in the store, and that it downloads correctly and works? Remember that until it goes live in the store, you can't download it and check it. If it's going up for sale in multiple versions of the store (i.e., different countries), do you have people with accounts in all those countries that can check that it went live?

Things to Worry About on Launch Day

If you've done everything right, you should be able to sit back and bask in the glory of a successfully launched product. If things have gone pear-shaped, you hopefully have contingency plans in place so at least you know what direction to panic in. If worst comes to worst, you can always pull the app out of the store.

I know that, in spite of the last week fire-drill, the day that my iOS app went live in the store was one of the proudest in my life. As I type this, I can look up and see a framed copy of the marketing poster for the app, which hangs in my office at home. I sincerely hope that your launch day is as happy and trouble-free as ours was.

Things to Worry About in the Month After Launch

Most likely, you'll already be deep into your 1.1 or 2.0 project planning. But this will also be the time that your first bug reports will start trickling in. My project was a bit of an aberration, in that it required customers to install a new release of the backend server product, something we knew any of our customers were unlikely to do in the first few months of the release. So we knew that, literally, no one would actually be using our software until close to our 2.0 release.

It's unlikely that you'll be in the same boat. And, in fact, we found some problems that were introduced by a maintenance release of the backend, which broke the mobile clients. So, even though no one was using the clients, we had to do a 1.1 release (and a subsequent 1.1.1 release) in the months following launch.

As part of your initial (and ongoing) discussions with your support and production groups, you should have a plan in place for what should go out in follow-up releases, and when they should be released. The App Store gives you a great deal of latitude to get critical bug fixes out to the users quickly, but the existing groups are unlikely to want you to "cowboy" fixes into the Store without proper release controls.

The App Store is the primary way to distribute applications, but it may not fit every customer's needs. In the next chapter, we'll look at alternate (legal) means of distributing applications.

CHAPTER 7

Distributing Enterprise iOS Applications

If you're distributing apps for sale to end users, the process is fairly straightforward. You sign up for an iOS developer account, create a development provisioning profile, build your app and test it on devices set up for debugging, create a distribution provisioning profile, build and archive your app, and upload it to the store.

This model works well for consumer products developed by an individual or small group, but there are other ways to do things that will assist you when developing applications in the enterprise.

Testing Applications with Ad Hoc Profiles

In a large organization, a lot of people may want to get their hands on your application before launch. Obviously, there's your QA group, but also people from sales and marketing, internationalization, performance testing, and beta customers. Having them all come over to your desk to hook their devices up to your Mac and deploy the app with XCode can quickly become a nightmare. Toward the end of our 2.0 release, we had over 40 devices being used internally for testing.

The way to get around this is by using an Ad Hoc profile. An Ad Hoc signed app contains the UDID of every device that is allowed to run the application. Once a UDID is included in the app, you can send them the packaged IPA file, and they can drag it right into iTunes and install it to the device. Better yet, as you will see, we can automate the process so that they can directly download it from the build server.

The first step is to add all the devices into the iOS Provisioning Portal (Figure 7-1). This can be a fairly painful process, as UDIDs are pretty long. The easiest way to do this is to have your testers fire up iTunes, select their docked device, click on the Serial Number field (which will toggle it to displaying the UDID), and hit copy (Command or Alt-C, depending on the OS), shown in Figure 7-2.

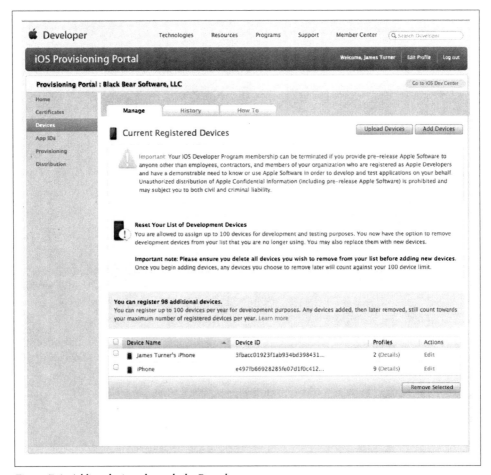

Figure 7-1. Adding devices through the Portal

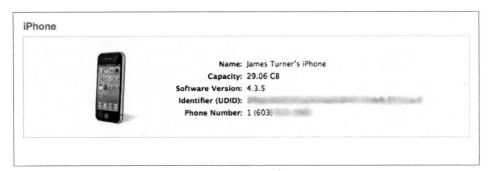

Figure 7-2. Copying the UDID from iTunes

Once they send you the UDID, you add it to the device list along with a name. Now you can generate an Ad Hoc profile using the devices, by selecting the side provisioning tab on the portal, and then the distribution tab on the top (Figure 7-3).

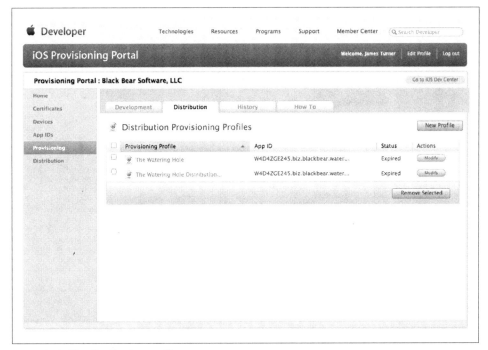

Figure 7-3. The distribution profile page

Finally, click on New Profile, choose Ad Hoc as the distribution method, pick a good profile name, associate it with your app via the app ID, and select the devices to be included in the profile (Figure 7-4). Once you have submitted the form, you'll be returned to the distribution profile page, and can refresh and then download the new profile.

Once you've downloaded the profile, you can double-click on it and it will be installed into your keychain and be available from XCode. You need to set your project up to do an Ad Hoc build, which involves a number of steps which are well documented on Apple's iOS developer's portal, but I'll summarize them here. You need to create an Ad Hoc configuration in your project, set the entitlements file for it, and set the code signing identity for the configuration to be the new Ad Hoc profile. Now you can archive your project (the same as if you were going to upload it to the App Store), then use the share button to create an IPA file that you can distribute to your testers as you like.

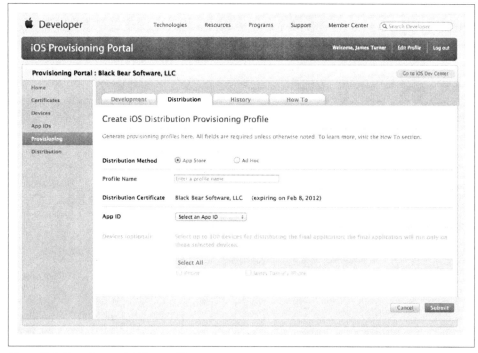

Figure 7-4. Creating an Ad Hoc profile

The first time through, this isn't so bad. But what happens the next time someone wants to add a device? You need to go back to the portal, add the devices, add the devices to the profile, regenerate the profile, download the profile and install it in your keychain, edit the application, and select the new version of the profile in the Ad Hoc configuration as the code signing identity, rearchive the app, and distribute it. And then, probably, pour yourself a stiff drink. Now imagine doing that a couple of times a week!

One way I try to avoid some of the madness is to insist that new device additions be bundled up in groups, so that I can add 5 or 10 at a time rather than in onesie-twosies. Of course, if the VP of sales needs to be added so that he can give a demo, you'll probably have to bend your policy. Another way you can spare yourself some pain is to incorporate the creation of an Ad Hoc image into your automated build processes. The magic command you need to add to the build is:

```
/usr/bin/xcrun -sdk iphoneos PackageApplication \
-v appfile -o ipafile --embed mobileprovisionfile
```

So, for example, the Buggy Whip folks might say (assuming that the app file was in the *build* folder, the profile in the *certs* folder, and that the resulting *.ipa* file should be placed in the *dist* folder):

```
/usr/bin/xcrun -sdk iphoneos PackageApplication \
-v build/BuggyWhipChat.app -o dist/BuggyWhipChat.ipa \
--embed certs/BuggyWhipChatAdHoc.mobileprovision
```

You also need to make sure that if you build your application on a different machine (such as in the scenario described in Chapter 3), that you also import the new profile into the keychain on the build machine—otherwise it will fail.

Now, assuming that the build process deposits the *.ipa* file in a location that the test community can access, they can simply grab the newest copy of the file and install it with iTunes.

A Better Mousetrap for Ad Hoc Infrastructure

Once you've been around the merry-go-round a few times with the Ad Hoc process, it will grow tiresome—trust me. Fortunately, there are now alternate ways to make your job easier. The two best known are TestFlight and Apperian (which will be discussed in the next chapter). I've been using TestFlight with great success, so that is what I'll talk about here, but Apperian is supposed to work in much the same way. Additionally, you can roll your own version of TestFlight and deploy an Ad Hoc build to your own web server, using tools such as iOS Beta Builder and Hockey, but TestFlight offers such a (free) soup to nuts solution that I'd be hesitant not to use it unless you are philosophically opposed to a cloud-based solution.

TestFlight doesn't eliminate the pain of having to create new Ad Hoc profiles and rebuild the app when devices are added, but it does get you out of the business of having to collect the UDIDs, and notify the testers when there are new versions of the app. It also lets testers install the app without needing to run iTunes—they can do it directly from the device. Here, in a nutshell, is how it works.

You begin by going to *http://testflightapp.com* and registering (Figure 7-5). Once you've registered, you can upload the Ad Hoc IPA file to TestFlight, and TestFlight will automatically cross-reference the UDID numbers embedded in the Ad Hoc profile with known devices that have been registered with TestFlight. You can then add these people to your test team with a single click. Now when you upload new versions of your app to TestFlight, they will automatically receive emails telling them to update, and if they open the email on their device, they'll get a link that will do it automatically without needing to sync to iTunes.

Even better, you can provide a short URL to new testers, and if they browse to the page on their devices, they can self-register for testing. You still get to approve them—and best of all, you get a copy of their UDID, so you can just paste it right into the portal. If you have a lot of people at once, you can even download a file with a list of all the UDIDs and device names, which you can then upload into the portal.

Figure 7-5. TestFlight home page

Now, here's the really slick part. TestFlight has a public API that lets you automatically upload new versions of the app from your build process. You get an API key on the TestFlight site, and then incorporate it into your build using HTTP. For example, using *curl*, you could do it like this:

```
curl http://testflightapp.com/api/builds.xml \
    -F file=@BuggyWhip.ipa \
    -F api_token='asfasjfaslfaslfkasldfja' \
    -F team_token='asdfkasdfsdflkajsaksdjfh' \
    -F notes='<releasenotes' \
    -F notify=True\
    -F distribution_lists='QA-People'
```

This uploads the *BuggyWhip.ipa* file using the assigned api and team tokens you got from the TestFlight site, taking the notes for the release from a file called *releasenotes* and sending a notification to everyone on the TestFlight QA-People team. I've gone so far as to have my build script automatically pull the last commit message out of the source control system and use that as the release note message, so the testers know what bug fixes or features might be in the latest build.

I can't recommend strongly enough that you consider using TestFlight (or a similar service) for managing your test infrastructure. It has made my life—and the life of my testers—significantly less stressful.

Advanced Testflight-Fu

Once you have TestFlight spinning builds out to your beta users, you can use the newly released TestFlight SDK to take things to the next level. Specifically, you can let Test-Flight track all of your test user's sessions, capture logs and checkpoint information, and even deliver crash reports to you.

All you need to do is to follow the directions on the TestFlight site that document how to enable the SDK in your app. If you do nothing else other than link in the library and make the initialization call in your app delegate startup, you'll get start and end of session timestamps, crash reports, and the contents of anything sent to the console log. The one important caveat is that you should put all of the TestFlight calls inside compile-time conditionalizations and make sure they are not included in the production (App Store) build of your app.

Enterprise Distribution

If you are developing an application strictly for in-house use, or for one specific customer, there is another type of distribution that sidesteps the App Store: an enterprise distribution profile. You get one by registering as an Enterprise developer (which is more expensive). Once you have registered, you can create enterprise provisioning profiles, which can be used to create applications that anyone in your organization can install, either via iTunes, over the air from a website, or via the iPhone Configuration Utility.

Before you get all excited about giving Apple and the iTunes store the finger, and distributing all your applications as Enterprise applications, you should know that whenever an application is installed with an Enterprise signing identity, the device does a round-trip handshake to the Mother Ship in Cupertino, and authorizes. I'm pretty sure that if Apple starts to see thousands of people from all over the place authorizing your app, your Enterprise license is going to get yanked pronto, and you may get a call from the Men in Suits. So be a good developer, and leave Enterprise distribution for honest-to-goodness internal Enterprise apps.

That having been said, Enterprise licenses make a lot of sense if you plan to have a lot of beta testers of your applications, and they all work for your company. The Enterprise license requires that all devices that run an Enterprise-licensed version of the App be owned by employees of your company, and third-parties can only use the application if an employee physically has possession of the device at all times.

In our case, we started out using a standard Ad Hoc license, and then just in the past week (as of when I wrote these words), switched over to an Enterprise license for all of our internal users. This had two big benefits, because we were approaching our magic 100 device limit on the Ad Hoc license, and because I was spending a significant part of my week adding new UDID entries to the iTunes provisioning portal as people wanted to join the party.

You can use Enterprise licenses solely for in-house distribution, but inside of that limitation they are very flexible. You can even use tools like Testflight to distribute Enterprise-signed applications, or set up your own web server with the appropriate meta-data to let your users download them directly in-house. Of course, you can also distribute it via email and iTunes, the same way you can distribute Ad Hoc binaries.

A Gotcha With Enterprise-Based Development

One problem you're almost certainly going to run into while using an Enterprise license to do beta-testing of apps you plan to deliver to the App Store is *key interference*. If you've done enough iOS development, you've almost certainly run into issues where you had an old, stale provisioning profile hanging around or multiple copies of your development key in your keychain, and you couldn't sign your app because XCode complained.

This problem comes home to roost if you have both an Enterprise license (which, re-member, you can't use to sign apps for the App Store) and a normal distribution license. The problem is that they will be signed by different keys, but the keys will both have your organization as the name of the key. This confuses XCode, which thinks that you can only have one key at any one time assigned to a given entity. The solution to this problem involves creating multiple keychains using the Keychain Access tool, each one of which has the key and certificates for the Enterprise or Distribution profile, but not the other. You also need to make sure that neither key or certificate appears in the login or system keychains.

Another issue is that you can't use the same bundle identifier for both builds, because Apple won't let provisioning profiles for different developers share the same bundle identifier. Unfortunately, Apple requires that you use two entirely different developer accounts for the Enterprise and App store profiles. You need to work around this by dynamically changing the bundle identifier based on the build type. I have specific build configurations for each (one called App Store, and one called Enterprise). You can see an example in Figure 7-6.

I create a user defined variable called `APPLICATION_BUNDLE_IDENTIFIER`, with different values for the different build configurations (Figure 7-7). Having done this, you can now use a special hack to create both Enterprise and App Store builds. You need to set `Expand Build Setting in Info.plist File` to Yes, as well.

Now, in your app's *info.plist* file, change the `Bundle Identifier` to `${APPLICATION_BUNDLE_IDENTIFIER}` (shown in Figure 7-8). Now, depending on whether you specify the App Store or Enterprise build configuration (which is available as a parameter in *xcodebuild*), you will get a different bundle identifier.

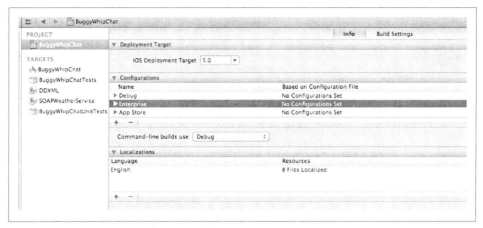

Figure 7-6. Multiple build configurations for Enterprise and App store

Figure 7-7. Creating a user-defined bundle identifier

Icon file	◎ ◎	String	Icon.png
▶ Icon files		Array	(6 items)
Bundle identifier		String	${APPLICATION_BUNDLE_IDENTIFIER}
InfoDictionary version		String	6.0
Bundle name		String	${PRODUCT_NAME}
Bundle OS Type code		String	APPL
Bundle creator OS Type code		String	????

Figure 7-8. Parameterizing the Info.plist file

You still need to tell XCode which keychain to use, however. You do this using another build setting that you can customize to the build target: the Other Code Signing Flags setting. By adding a keychain argument, you can tell XCode which keychain to use for which build (Figure 7-9).

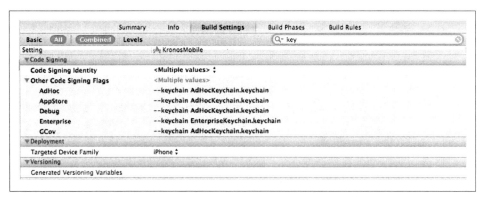

Figure 7-9. Setting the build keychain

The Long Haul

If you need to get your apps in the hands of third parties, the limited ways of distributing iOS apps can present a real challenge to long term maintenance of your app. In the next (and final) chapter, we'll examine some of those, and the strategies to overcome them.

CHAPTER 8

Long Term Maintenance of iOS Enterprise Applications

So, you've got an app in the store, people are starting to download and use it, and since you read this book from end to end, it went without a hitch and you're a hero at your company. Alas, your job has just begun. Now you have to support that sucker!

Of course, this is true of any software that has to actually be put in the hands of end users. Wouldn't life be so much easier without them? But, since you have them, you're going to need to deal with them in the long term. This presents one particular challenge for enterprise developers, and it's what this chapter is all about.

If your application connects to some resource in the cloud that's under your control, you can close this book and crack open a beverage of your choice. But if it connects to a backend server that isn't under your control, and which may exist at multiple version levels at the same time, read on.

A classic example of the first scenario is Salesforce. Individual customers don't install the Salesforce server—they use the common one in the cloud, and it is always at a given API level and server version. If Salesforce wants to release a new iPhone app, all they have to do is make sure that it lines up with one of the current versions of the API living on their servers, and they're golden.

But what about a scenario where your application is going to have to connect to multiple different versions of the server? In the case of the app I developed, our customers can take a year or more to actually place a new server version into production use, so we were facing the very real possibility of having to support 4 or 5 years worth of different APIs as we enhanced the backend functionality to add new features to the app.

No problem, you say: just have the users install the right version of the app for the API version they connect to. Sounds good, but remember that with the App Store, you can only have one version of the application available for download at any one time, and it can be automatically updated if they connect to iTunes. So short of telling customers not to upgrade their app, you have no way to keep them from downloading a new, incompatible version. And worse, that means that you have no way of distributing bug fixes to them. So, to quote the old American Express commercials, what will you do?

Option 1: The Perpetually Compatible Application

One way to approach the problem is to keep your application perpetually back-compatible with every version of the API that has ever existed. It's not impossible, especially if you're clever about it. What you want to avoid is sprinkling your API integration code with conditionals everywhere. A more modular approach is to use a protocol to define your API functions, and use different implementing classes to handle different API versions. Then on first connect to the server, you can figure out which API version you're talking to, and provision the correct implementing class to talk to it.

On the surface, this doesn't look like a bad option, at least until you start thinking through to the next level of code. Suppose version 1.0 of our BuggyWhipChat application connects to version 1.0 of the backend API, and supports features A and B. Version 2.0 of the app connects to version 1.1 of the backend API, and supports A, B, and C. You don't know at first glance if the application is going to connect to a 1.0 or 1.1 backend, so you have to conditionalize your UI and business logic—not just your API interface code—to handle either possibility. It can get even worse when features on a single screen have to be conditionalized. You can end up with an app that is essentially thousands of "if" statements flying in close formation.

Now multiply that times 5 or even 10 different backend API versions, and you can imagine how messy your application code can end up. Depending on how aggressive you are about sunsetting support for older server versions, it can quickly become a nightmare, particularly for testing, as you'll have to regression-test all new application versions against all the supported server versions.

And think about what happens if you do sunset support for an old server version. What happens to the customers who refuse to upgrade? The next time their application updates from the App Store, it will break. I suppose that's one strategy to get your customers to keep up their support contracts, but it may not be a very politically popular one.

(Non-)Option 2: The Perpetually Compatible Server

A little thought will make it clear that trying to place the compatibility requirement on the server side is a non-starter. Remember, the problem is not with an out-of-date client, since we can pretty much assure that the client will always be the latest version (and enforce it with upgrade messages inside the app that force the user to upgrade before proceeding). The problem is with an out-of-date server, which can't support all the new or changed features of the app.

There's no way to build forward-compatibility into a server, and the client will still have to conditionalize on what comes back in the payload from the server. So, we're back to square one.

Option 3: App Store Version Roulette

What you'd really like to do is to match a specific server version to a specific app version, so that you keep down the conditional code inside your app and reduce your testing matrix nightmare. Your Android brethren have this base covered, because you can directly download Android applications to the phone without going through an app store, at least with most carriers. But along with the added security of the iTunes App Store, you also lose the ability to directly install apps, unless you're a developer.

What you can do is place multiple products in the app store, each basically a version of the application specific to a given server backend. So, in essence, you'd have Buggy Whip Chat for Server Version 1.0, Buggy Whip Chat for Server Version 2.0, etc. This allows you to have customized maintenance releases inside of each API version, but make a clean cutoff on the functionality axis.

There are a few problems with this technique, alas. First off, you've now shifted the responsibility of applying conditionalization logic on to the end user. They may have no idea what version of the backend software they are connecting. This means that their IT department is going to have to communicate this information to the users, and then update the information if they ever upgrade their server software.

More alarmingly, you're now potentially spamming the App Store with multiple versions of the same product. How many versions of the same app will Apple allow before they pull the plug, perhaps without notice? It took a trip to WWDC and a one-on-one with senior management of the App Store to get an answer for my company; you may not have the time and resources to do the same.

Option 4: Exotic Distribution Methods

If the customer base is small enough and the revenue from the app high enough, you might consider doing a custom Enterprise version of the app for each customer. In other words, have each customer apply for an Enterprise provisioning certificate, send it to you, and use it to compile a customer version of the app that the customer can have their employees directly download.

Another alternative is to use a boutique app store. It isn't well advertised, but Apple actually has a spin-off company called Apperian, which allows enterprises to create private-label app stores. It still requires an enterprise-provisioned application, but it provides a more App Store feeling experience.

Both of these strategies allow tight control of which application version will be associated with which server backend, but at the cost of having to provide concierge-level support to the customer base. This may be practical if you have a small customer base with lots of users in each one, but fails badly if you have hundreds or thousands of customers.

Option 5: The Swiss Army App

What we'd really like to have happen is that the application would contact the server, and download the appropriate version of the application from there. But Apple's T&Cs prohibit the downloading of binary code into applications, so you're out of luck there. Apple does allow you to download scripting code, so if you can make your app work with something like LUA or JavaScript, you may have an out, although it's unlikely.

There's one final approach you can try to crack this nut. If you're willing to have your code base and binary size swell linearly with the number of API versions you support, you can duplicate your code base every time you spin off a new server version, change all the class names to have the new server version appended to the end, and then have your initial startup code choose which version of the application to run. In other words, you have a single application which is really multiple applications wrapped together with a crunchy shell. Assuming that nothing from one version steps on another version's toes, that the binary size doesn't get out of hand, and that you can manage any shared resource issues correctly, this may be the easier solution to swallow.

Welcome to the Club, We Have Jackets

We've come to the end of our Enterprise journey (hopefully not a five-year mission, at least for the first release...). By now, I hope you have a proper respect for the challenges that enterprise developers in the Apple world face, but haven't been scared off from proceeding further. There is no question that Apple has made enterprise iOS applications a difficult product to produce, but it can be done, and done well.

The good news is that all signs point to better sailing ahead. Apple continues to add features to the SDK and the marketplace that make it easier to develop and distribute iOS application to enterprise customers. There is even hope that we may see direct B2B distribution capabilities some day—the launch of the volume licensing program is a clear indicator of that.

So in conclusion, and to paraphrase Mary Schmich's famous Chicago Tribune column, push the bounds of the App Store, but don't let it get you banned. Fight non-applicable corporate policies, but don't let it get you fired. And remember to wear sunscreen.

About the Author

James Turner is a freelance journalist and developer who has recently spent more than a year developing an enterprise iOS application for a major software ISV. He is a contributing editor for oreilly.com, and has written for publications as diverse as the Christian Science Monitor, Processor, Linuxworld Magazine, Developer.com and WIRED Magazine. In addition to his shorter writing, he has also written two books on Java Web Development (*MySQL & JSP Web Applications* and *Struts: Kick Start*, both by Sams). He is the former Senior Editor of LinuxWorld Magazine and Senior Contributing Editor for Linux Today. He has also spent more than 30 years as a software engineer and system administrator, and currently works as a Senior Software Engineer for a company in the Boston area. His past employers include the MIT Artificial Intelligence Laboratory, Xerox AI Systems, Solbourne Computer, Interleaf, the Christian Science Monitor, and contracting positions at BBN and Fidelity Investments. He is a committer on the Apache Jakarta Struts project and served as the Struts 1.1B3 release manager. He lives in a 200-year-old Colonial farmhouse in Derry, NH with his wife and son. He is an open water diver and instrument-rated private pilot, as well as an avid science fiction fan.

Get even more for your money.

Join the O'Reilly Community, and register the O'Reilly books you own. It's free, and you'll get:

- $4.99 ebook upgrade offer
- 40% upgrade offer on O'Reilly print books
- Membership discounts on books and events
- Free lifetime updates to ebooks and videos
- Multiple ebook formats, DRM FREE
- Participation in the O'Reilly community
- Newsletters
- Account management
- 100% Satisfaction Guarantee

Signing up is easy:

1. **Go to: oreilly.com/go/register**
2. **Create an O'Reilly login.**
3. **Provide your address.**
4. **Register your books.**

Note: English-language books only

To order books online:
oreilly.com/store

For questions about products or an order:
orders@oreilly.com

To sign up to get topic-specific email announcements and/or news about upcoming books, conferences, special offers, and new technologies:
elists@oreilly.com

For technical questions about book content:
booktech@oreilly.com

To submit new book proposals to our editors:
proposals@oreilly.com

O'Reilly books are available in multiple DRM-free ebook formats. For more information:
oreilly.com/ebooks

Spreading the knowledge of innovators   **oreilly.com**

The information you need, when and where you need it.

With Safari Books Online, you can:

Access the contents of thousands of technology and business books

- Quickly search over 7000 books and certification guides
- Download whole books or chapters in PDF format, at no extra cost, to print or read on the go
- Copy and paste code
- Save up to 35% on O'Reilly print books
- **New!** Access mobile-friendly books directly from cell phones and mobile devices

Stay up-to-date on emerging topics before the books are published

- Get on-demand access to evolving manuscripts.
- Interact directly with authors of upcoming books

Explore thousands of hours of video on technology and design topics

- Learn from expert video tutorials
- Watch and replay recorded conference sessions

Spreading the knowledge of innovators   safari.oreilly.com

CPSIA information can be obtained at www.ICGtesting.com
Printed in the USA
BVOW050552141211

278299BV00003B/2/P